RAILWAYS AND TRAMWAYS
OF THE
ISLE OF MAN

• A PAST and PRESENT COMPANION •

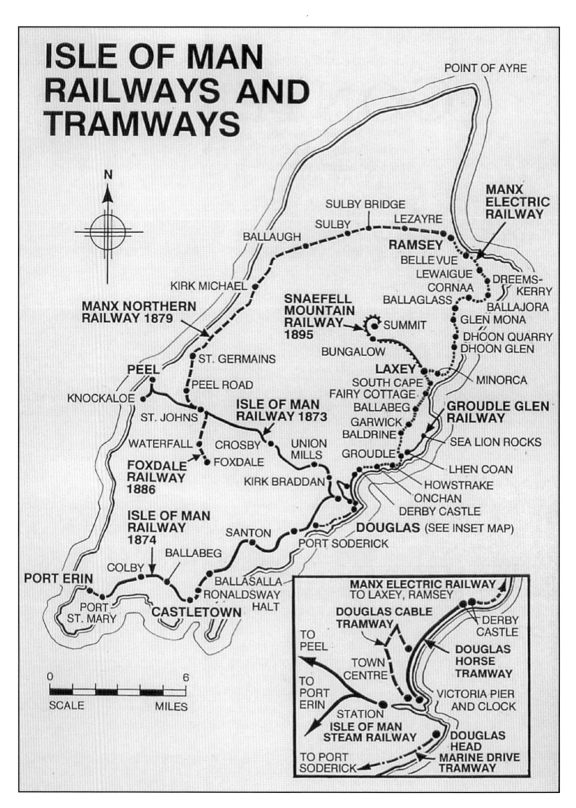

Map of railway systems of the Isle of Man, showing locations pictured or mentioned in the text. *Alan Palmer*

RAILWAYS AND TRAMWAYS OF THE
ISLE OF MAN

·A PAST AND PRESENT COMPANION·

Ted Gray

·RAILWAY HERITAGE·
from
The NOSTALGIA *Collection*

Sir Norman Wisdom, possibly the Isle of Man's most famous inhabitant, was invited to contribute a Foreword to this book, but, now in his 90s, he didn't feel up to the task. However, being very interested in vintage transport, especially cars, he was happy to send this personal message.

First published in 2008

British Library Cataloguing in Publication Data

A catalogue record for this book is available from the British Library.

ISBN 978 1 85895 196 6

Past & Present Publishing Ltd
The Trundle
Ringstead Road
Great Addington
Kettering
Northants NN14 4BW

Tel/Fax: 01536 330588
email: sales@nostalgiacollection.com
Website: www.nostalgiacollection.com

Printed and bound in the Czech Republic

Half title The Isle of Man Railway's youngest steam locomotive, No 16 *Mannin*, stands by the water tower outside the Port Erin shed in August 1938. Mannin was purchased from Beyer Peacock in 1926, the first new locomotive since *Kissack* arrived in 1910. Larger than its predecessors, it was ordered specifically to haul the heavy trains of the south line, and rid the company of the costly practice of double-heading. Consequently *Mannin* spent nearly all of her working life on the Port Erin line. The locomotive was named after an ancient name for the island. Withdrawn in 1964, she is still in Port Erin, a permanent exhibit in the museum. *GH*

Title page The IMR company crest survives on the gateposts of the station building at Douglas. *EG*

Past and Present

A Past & Present book
from
The NOSTALGIA Collection

CONTENTS

The extension of the Manx Electric Railway to Laxey was completed by July 1894, and car 7 with trailer 15 is seen on the opening day, posed on the curve at Port Jack. The six cars of the 4-9 series were purchased to add to the original three used on the short 1893 service to Groudle, and a new power station to provide additional current was built at Laxey. The cars then carried the title 'Douglas & Laxey Electric Tramway'. The steam-roller is evidence that the roadway was then unfinished. The imposing Douglas Bay Hotel once dominated the skyline at the north end of the promenade.

Today the new offices of Skandia rise on the former site of the hotel. Winter saloon 21 and trailer 41 head for Ramsey on 7 June 2006. *M&P/EG*

The line from St John's to Peel entered the town via the Mill Road crossing, where there was a water tower with a small engine shed alongside. In this 1954 view locomotive No 12 *Hutchinson* stands by the water tower, with the engine shed hidden from view behind it. The station buildings and goods shed lie beyond.

Today much of the former platform area is occupied by a car park and boat yard, but the water tower remains, together with a short length of track, crossing gates, and a signal rescued from the Ramsey line – a creditable effort organised by the Peel Heritage Trust. *AV/EG*

INTRODUCTION

Until the unprecedented tourist boom of the late Victorian era, the Isle of Man was a sparsely populated land of fishermen, farmers and miners. The creation of the island's land-based transport systems resulted from the demand of the many thousands of summer visitors, attracted by the pleasant climate and charming scenery, for a means to carry them to places of interest inland or around the coast. Most of the tourists came from the north-west of England, generally arriving by ship at Douglas, the principal town, so it is not surprising that the first railways and tramways were constructed to link Douglas with other parts of the island.

Within a relatively short period of a little over 20 years (1873-96) no fewer than nine different passenger transport systems were established, often with funds provided by entrepreneurs from the mainland, and using equipment supplied by north-west manufacturers. Steady progress during the early years of the 20th century was interrupted by the war of 1914-18, when the island was used for the internment of foreign nationals, and again during the period of the Second World War, during both of which there was a complete absence of holiday-makers.

In the post-war world of the 1950s it became clear that the increasing popularity of air travel and package holidays would force the island to rely less on seasonal visitors. In addition, the growth in private car ownership meant that island residents used public transport to a much lesser degree than formerly. Inevitably, passenger receipts fell drastically, and the island's railways suffered from a lack of investment. However, against the odds, with Government intervention and a great deal of support from voluntary agencies, much has survived.

The Manx Electric Railway, despite passing through a difficult period in the 1970s, remains intact, as does the Snaefell Mountain Railway. On the steam railway, although the lines to Peel and Ramsey have long since closed, the south line between Douglas and Port Erin continues to operate on a seasonal basis, while the horse-drawn trams still carry visitors along the Douglas promenade. The Groudle Glen Railway has been rescued from dereliction and splendidly restored by volunteers. Similarly, enthusiastic amateurs have re-instated the Laxey Mines Railway, and established the Orchid Line, a miniature railway that operates within the grounds of the Wild Life Park near Sulby. So, the island still has much to attract lovers of vintage transport.

ACKNOWLEDGEMENTS

I am particularly indebted to Richard Dodge of the Manx Electric Railway Society; David Packer, Dr Chris Thornburn and Tony Wilson (Travel Lens) for their generous assistance with photographs; and the authors of books listed in the Bibliography for their research and expertise. Illustrations are credited to the original photographers where known, using the following abbreviations: A. D. Packer (ADP), Arthur Kirby (AKK), Adrian Vaughan (AV), Dr Chris Thornburn (CCT), the collection of the late David Bailey (DB), G. A. Dean (GAD), G. Harrop (GH), H. B. Priestley (HBP), Ken Hassall and Steve Dearden (KH&SD), Ken Nunn (KN), Manx Press Pictures (MPP), Mather & Platt (M&P), the late Robert F. Mack (RFM), R. Hargreaves (RH), Real Photographs (RP), S. R. Keig (SRK), Travel Lens Photographics (TLP), Transport Treasury (N. Forrest) (TT), Valentine of Dundee (V) and the late W. A. Camwell (WAC). Photographs by the author are credited as EG, and apologies are offered for any inadvertent omissions.

Abbreviations used in the text are DHMD (Douglas Head Marine Drive), FR (Foxdale Railway), IMR (Isle of Man Railway), MER (Manx Electric Railway), MNR (Manx Northern Railway),and SMR (Snaefell Mountain Railway). The sections in the book have been arranged in the order of opening dates of the various undertakings from 1873 to 1896, except in the case of the Manx Northern (1879) and Foxdale Railway (1886), where, as both connected with the Peel line at St John's, and as both were eventually absorbed by the IMR, it seemed sensible to deal as geographically encountered.

Ted Gray
Ramsey
Isle of Man

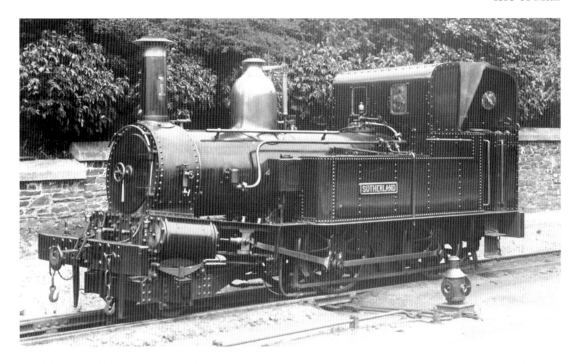

The Isle of Man Railway Company favoured the products of the Beyer Peacock locomotive works in Gorton, Manchester, and for the opening of the Peel line ordered three 2-4-0 side tank engines. The first of the three,

named *Sutherland* after the Duke of Sutherland, first Chairman of the Company and a director of the London & North Western Railway, was delivered to the island in March 1873, in good time for trial runs to take place before the official opening. On arrival it sported a green livery.

Sutherland remained in service until withdrawn in 1964, after which the locomotive spent many years in store, latterly in the Port Erin Museum, until removed and restored in time for the Isle of Man Railway's 'STEAM 125' celebrations in 1998. The photographs, dated 1926 and 1998, were both taken outside the steam shed by the platform ends. *KN/EG*

Isle of Man Railway: Douglas to St John's

The first passenger railway in the Isle of Man was the 11½-mile 3-foot-gauge line across the centre of the island, connecting Douglas in the east with the fishing port of Peel in the west, which opened for traffic on 1 July 1873. The first station at Douglas was a relatively modest timber structure, replaced in 1892 by a magnificent edifice of red brick, with an adjoining building to accommodate the administrative offices. The main entrance opened on to the harbourside, but staircases and a second pedestrian entrance were constructed in 1889 for the benefit of passengers arriving from the town centre. Such extravagance was unusual for a narrow gauge railway. The gilded domes surmounting the side-entrance arch on Peel Road are well-known landmarks, though the Grecian urns on the brick piers have gone, as seen in these views from 1950 and 2006. *RFM/EG*

All the buildings survive today. The former administrative offices are currently occupied by the Customs & Excise department and an insurance company, and part of the booking hall now accommodates a café. *EG*

Douglas station is seen first at the opening of the Peel line, 1 July 1873. Locomotive No 1 *Sutherland*, decorated with a banner that reads 'DOUGLAS & PEEL UNITED', heads a train of four-wheeled carriages, whose differing paint styles indicate class. Note the open wagons on the track with half-round sleepers, and the original station building.

The second picture, from 1910, shows that the timber building has been removed (sold off as a sports pavilion) and replaced by the more substantial red-brick structure. Locomotives Nos 7 *Tynwald* and 9 *Douglas* stand on the release road waiting their turn of duty.

The station was further improved by the addition of awnings over the main platforms and the enclosure of the concourse area by the booking hall, illustrated in the third view, dated 29 June 1965. Locomotive No 8 *Fenella* moves along the release road, having just brought in a train from Ramsey.

Finally, *Fenella* is seen again, this time in 2006, restored to working order after a long period of disuse. Withdrawn in 1968, the locomotive was purchased in 1978 by the Isle of Man Railway & Tramway Preservation Society, together with other engines and items of rolling-stock, and has since been completely refurbished. The platform canopies have gone, sadly dismantled in 1978 to avoid cost of repair and maintenance. *GAD (2)/EG (2)*

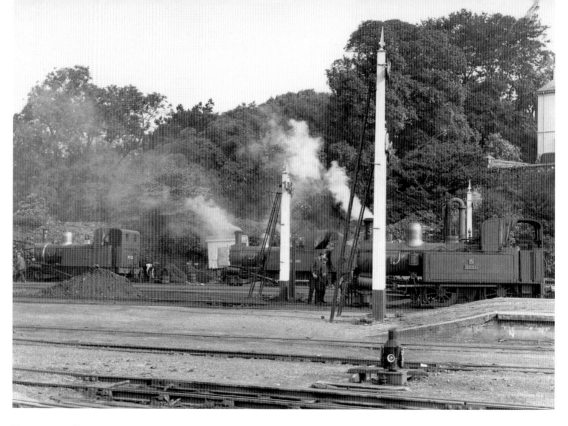

For steam railway enthusiasts, morning preparations outside the steam shed at Douglas were a time of endless fascination. When all three lines to Peel, Port Erin and Ramsey were in operation, the scene was always busy. At the outer sheds, only one locomotive would usually be in evidence, but at Douglas, the hub of the network, three or four engines were in steam. In the first view, taken in July 1965, Nos 13 *Kissack*, 11 *Maitland*, and 5 *Mona* are being prepared for their first duties of the day. *Kissack* and *Maitland* were named after company board members, while *Mona* is an old name for the Isle of Man. At some point, in addition to her chimney numbers, *Mona* acquired small brass numbers mounted above the nameplate on the tank sides, but by the late 1950s carried the number on the left side only. (No 12 *Hutchinson* was similarly fitted with tank-side numbers, which it carried until the 1980 rebuild. No other engines were so treated.)

Despite the loss of the Peel and Ramsey lines (closed in 1968), there are still three locomotives in steam in the second view. But the occasion is a special one – the centenary celebration of 1 July 1973. No 4 *Loch* (new for the

south line in 1874 and named after a respected island Governor) is preparing to haul a service train, while *Kissack* and No 10 *G. H. Wood* are scheduled to work the 3.45pm ten-coach non-stop centenary train from Port Erin to Douglas. *Kissack*'s 'headboard' was fixed on the rear because it was to be the leading engine on the return from Port Erin. Locomotives normally work chimney-first outwards from Douglas, bunker-first on return.

The third view is from the same weekend, with *Kissack* and *G. H. Wood* (the latter named after a former Company Secretary) gently simmering in an otherwise deserted scene, while the crews take a break. No 4 *Loch* is just visible inside the shed. The timetable on the south line at this time could be worked by three engines in steam, two based at Douglas and one at Port Erin. Note the old carriage outside the shed, used as a mess room by the engine men.

The current seasonal timetable requires only two engines to operate the service on the 15½-mile run. There are two morning and two afternoon departures from each terminus, trains crossing at Ballasalla. Visitors to the Douglas shed will usually see only one locomotive in steam at any one time. In the view from 7 September 2006, *Kissack* is being coaled by the fireman. The 'mess room' has gone, and a spare boiler stands in its place. Note also the fuel tank by the coal stack. *All EG*

This is Douglas station from the concourse end. In the Centenary Year (1973) several disused locomotives were hauled out of storage to be placed on display alongside the platform. By this time the lines to Peel and Ramsey had been abandoned, so the celebrations centred on the Port Erin line, which had opened in 1874. On the left, No 4 *Loch* leaves a train that has just arrived from Port Erin, while Nos 16 *Mannin*, 14 *Thornhill* and 3 *Pender*, all lifeless, shelter behind the palm trees. Douglas station was at this date, 2 July 1973, still reasonably intact.

Seen from the same spot on 7 September 2006, No 13 *Kissack* leaves its train to be coaled and watered at the shed. The canopies and the palm trees have gone, and the track layout is now on a much reduced scale. *Both EG*

This view, looking eastwards into the station from the signal box on 2 July 1972, illustrates the once vast extent of the Douglas station complex. The departure platforms for the former north lines were to the left, with the south line platform in the centre and the station buildings beyond. To the right was the goods yard. The end of the long carriage shed is on the extreme right. At this date much of the goods rolling-stock still survived, largely unused, as this once important feature of operations had dwindled. Only the centre platform was in use for railway passengers on the Port Erin line, the former north line platform having been relegated to serve as a car storage area, bringing in a little additional revenue from the competitors.

The view from the signal box ladder today is different, partly because the signal box itself has been re-sited in a different position, but mainly because the former goods yard area is now a parking lot for motor buses. The signalling system is different, too, having changed from semaphore to colour light and back to semaphore again in April 2005. *Both EG*

The view westwards from the platform ends has altered considerably. In the 'past' shot of 1 July 1973, the signal box can be seen in its original position, ideal for controlling entry and movement within the station complex. Behind it lies the long corrugated-iron carriage shed, within which were concealed a number of treasures. Locomotive No 4 *Loch* is seen backing down to what was then the centre platform to haul the 10.00am departure for Port Erin. The lines to Port Erin and Ramsey ran parallel, curving out of the picture to the far right.

With the signal box now redundant, but fortunately preserved and re-sited closer to the platform ends in 1999, the view in a westerly direction seems rather cramped and cluttered. Behind the signal box is now the new bus depot, washing plant and workshops. Only the trees and the railway workshops seem to have survived unmoved. The only other signal box on the system was at St John's. *Both EG*

Following the course of the original 1873 route to Peel, the line passed through Quarter Bridge to the first halt of note out of Douglas at Braddan, where a small wooden hut served as a booking office for passengers attending the popular Sunday open-air services at the nearby church. Long trains used to work out of Douglas, sometimes comprising as many as 18 coaches. As there was no loop at this point, some trains were worked with an engine at each end. At other times, the locomotive had to proceed to the next station, Union Mills, in order to run round its train.

In July 1972, the date of the second view, track and booking office were still in situ, though unused since 1968. The hut was eventually dismantled and removed for use at Colby on the south line.

Today the view from the overbridge presents a very different picture. The former trackbed along this length has been converted into an emergency access road, to enable traffic to the new Noble's Hospital to pass beneath the main road during the period of the TT motor cycle races. *TT/EG (2)*

The Peel line passed through Union Mills to reach Crosby, a small halt on the way to St John's. The station building was, like that at St John's, a designated 'Third Class' timber structure, incorporating a booking office, porters' room, general waiting room and ladies' waiting room. But the halt could also boast a goods shed and cattle dock. In this Victorian postcard view, looking east towards Douglas, potential passengers in their Sunday-best outfits contemplate the activities of the photographer.

Today the gate-keeper's stone lodge remains the only recognisable feature of the site. It appears to be reasonably well cared for, newly whitewashed for the benefit of walkers on the Steam Heritage Trail in this August 2006 view. *Commercial postcard/EG*

Right Westwards from Crosby station building was a generously long passing loop. Locomotive No 5 *Mona* is arriving with a five-coach Douglas-bound train, probably a combination of carriages from Peel and Ramsey, joined at St John's. *MPP*

Below This 1972 view after closure is looking in the opposite direction. In the left foreground are the points leading to the cattle dock, manure siding and goods shed. Track was lifted by the scrap metal merchants two years after this picture, and the station area was subsequently cleared and now forms part of a nearby school's playing fields. *EG*

It was often joked that St John's was the 'Clapham Junction' of the Isle of Man, for here three lines converged. In this 1953 view, looking westwards, the Peel line platforms are on the left, with a two-coach Peel to Douglas train in the charge of No 6 *Peveril* ready to depart. On the right No 3 *Pender* is marshalling a train for Ramsey. The sole connection between the Peel and Ramsey lines was behind the photographer. The third line, that to Foxdale, branched from the Ramsey line at a junction some distance beyond the station area, and curved behind the Railway Junction Hotel on the right to begin its climb on the steeply graded track to the mining village. Amazingly, there were once three stations in this small area: the IMR's original 1873 site (left and centre), the Manx Northern Railway's 1879 terminus (in the trees on the other side of the road), and the 1886 Foxdale branch station behind the trees by the hotel. All trains used the main site from 1904 when the IMR absorbed its competitors.

The Railway Junction Hotel is prominent in the 1956 view of *Pender* preparing to leave the centre platform with a train for Ramsey. On the closure of the railway, the hotel became privately owned and is now Sovereign House. An access road to the new St John's Primary School lies beyond the fence. *HBP/CCT/EG*

The former footbridge at the western end of St John's station complex once offered a fine vantage point for viewing operations, as here in 1939. The area tended to have sudden bursts of activity with the simultaneous arrival and departure of trains to and from Douglas, Peel and Ramsey. No 3 *Pender* is at the head of a Ramsey train with cattle trucks attached (left), No 12 *Hutchinson* hauls the Douglas-bound train (centre), while No 6 *Peveril* waits with a train for Peel (right). Both the last two trains have goods vans attached to the rear. The Foxdale line overbridge can be glimpsed in the distance. Peel and Ramsey trains were timed to leave together when the crossing gates were opened, and ran on parallel single tracks for some distance before the lines diverged.

The greater part of the station site is now an unsurfaced car park. *WAC/EG*

St John's might have remained a relatively unimportant wayside halt had not the Manx Northern Railway arrived on the scene as a consequence of the IMR's failure to build a line to Ramsey. The St John's station building of 1873 (left) seemed a modest provision for what came to be an important junction. In this 1965 view, the pair of railcars obtained from the County Donegal system in 1961 are negotiating the Station Road level crossing on arrival from Peel. The railcars were numbered 19 and 20 on the Donegal system, and retained these numbers in the Isle of Man.

The Central Hotel, prominent in the view, survives, now renamed 'The Farmers' Arms'. *MPP/EG*

The Foxdale Railway

After the completion of its line to Peel, the IMR turned its attention to the Douglas-Port Erin line, which it completed in the following year, 1874. The company had no plans to embark on a further venture to serve the north of the island. Consequently, the Manx Northern Railway Company was formed to construct a 16½-mile line from Ramsey to St John's, where a junction was to be made with the IMR. The new line opened in 1878. At first MNR trains terminated at St John's, but by 1881 through coaches were worked by being attached to the IMR's Peel-Douglas trains.

A scheme for yet another company to construct a line to serve the lead-mining area south of St John's came to fruition in 1886.

This third undertaking, the nominally independent Foxdale Railway, entered into an agreement with the MNR to work its 2½-mile branch. Ore from Foxdale was to be exported via Ramsey, while coal to power the pumping engines at the mines was to be carried in the opposite direction. The IMR was to play no part in what was forecast to be a very profitable enterprise, and the junction with the MNR Ramsey line was planned accordingly.

The FR's brick building at St John's reflected the optimism of the time, and was much more impressive than the IMR's timber structure. In later years it became the home of the St John's Station Master. When photographed in July 1972, a rake of abandoned ore wagons rested on track outside the former station.

The base of the water tower survives, though overgrown with ivy, as seen on 2 April 2007. The route beneath the bridge is now barred, and the houses beyond, which once backed on to the track, have acquired sections of the former line as garden extensions. The station building continues in use as a private dwelling house. *Both EG*

At Foxdale the station building was similarly substantial for such a small undertaking. No 1 *Sutherland* approaches the terminal stub in August 1939 with a train of empty ore wagons. Behind the station, tracks continued across the road to enter the mine premises. Alas, the great hopes of 1886 were not fulfilled, and within a few years dwindling traffic from the mines reduced income from the branch to a trifling amount. The FR went into liquidation, but the MNR was obliged to honour its commitment and continue its loss-making operation of the branch, a situation that led subsequently to the MNR's absorption by the IMR in 1904. Passenger services on the Foxdale branch were always sparse, usually consisting of a locomotive with one coach attached to a mixed train. Mining ceased altogether in 1911, and from mid-1912 the station became unstaffed, except for the few minutes between the arrival and departure of trains. By the 1920s the service had been reduced to two trains per day weekdays-only, the 14-minute journey from St John's being worked by the locomotive crew between other duties. The removal of the spoil heaps (the Foxdale 'deads') saw increased traffic on the branch in the period 1935-41, much material being required for road works and runway construction at two airfields in the north of the island. But by 1941, although occasional wartime requirements saw spasmodic workings on the branch, the

regular passenger service had been replaced by a bus. Thereafter, the line lay largely unused, and it was accepted that Foxdale was unlikely to generate any further traffic. It is believed that the last trains to negotiate the line ran in January 1962, probably tidying up the site and collecting spare wagons. The track remained in situ until the mid-1970s.

The station building became a private dwelling, then a youth club, and currently houses a display assembled by the Foxdale Heritage Trust. The grounds of the Foxdale Primary School (right) now encroach on the former station area, and a pathway (centre) follows the old railway formation towards St John's. *WAC/EG*

St John's to Peel

West of St John's the IMR and MNR lines ran in parallel for about half a mile, the latter passing the trailing point that connected the Foxdale branch to the Ramsey line until curving off northwards at Ballaleece. The Peel line continued westwards for a further 2½ miles, entering Peel Station via the Mill Road crossing. Peel station was located by the mouth of the River Neb, and arriving passengers enjoyed fine views over the harbour towards Peel Castle. Locomotives leaving their train would reverse to take on coal and water by the Mill Road crossing. No 6 *Peveril*, a regular on the Peel line, runs round its train on the 19 September 1956.

Although services on the Peel line ended in 1968, steam returned 30 years later in the shape of No 1 *Sutherland*, transported to the former station site by road as part of the celebrations to mark the 125th anniversary of the opening of the IMR. The car park having been cleared for the occasion, *Sutherland* was steamed on a length of temporary track, to the delight of youngsters who were able to enjoy footplate rides. It was particularly fitting that the locomotive that hauled the inaugural train to Peel in 1873 should have been chosen for this duty. *CCT/EG*

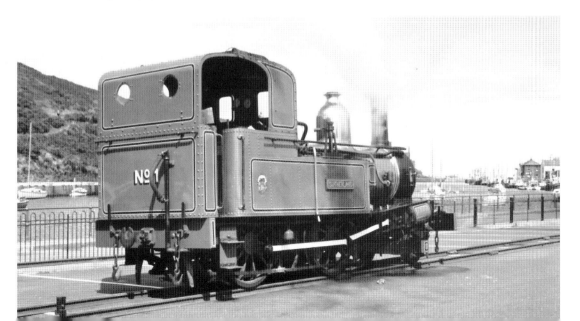

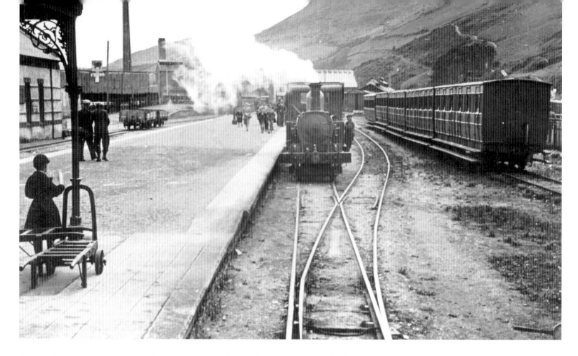

Above Viewed from the buffer stops at Peel, looking back towards St John's, this 1953 picture shows locomotive *Thornhill* arriving with a train from Douglas. Supplied in 1880 as Manx Northern's No 3, *Thornhill* was constructed to much the same design as the IMR's Beyer Peacock locomotives. It was named after the residence of the MNR Chairman, and was absorbed into the IMR fleet in 1905 as No 14. It was withdrawn from service in 1963, and has since been privately preserved in the north of the island. *HBP*

Below This 1958 scene, looking in the opposite direction, includes the more spacious station building, which replaced the original timber structure in 1908. At the platform No 5 *Mona* waits to leave with a train for Douglas. One of the railway's lorries may be noted parked under the awning. After the closure of the Peel line, the Railway Hotel beyond the buffer stops was renamed 'The Creek Inn'. *CCT*

Peel station building survived the closure of the railway, and subsequently served as a furniture store and upholsterer's shop, as well as housing the administrative offices of the Isle of Man Fishermen's Association.

In 1997 it was incorporated into Manx Heritage's 'House of Manannan', a museum of Manx life, the main entrance hall serving as a display area for temporary exhibitions. At the time of writing the items on display in the old station included a magnificent model of ex-Manx Northern locomotive *Caledonia*, which became No 15 in the IMR fleet. *Both EG*

Manx Northern Railway:
St John's to Ramsey

For the construction of its line to Ramsey, the Manx Northern Railway opted for a longer but more evenly graded west coast route. It was thought that the difficult terrain of the shorter east coast route would not be suitable for steam locomotives. The directors were not to know that 20 years later the Manx Electric Railway would successfully complete a line on the route they had rejected, thereby opening up competition for Ramsey traffic, and compounding the MNR's difficulties caused by falling receipts on the Foxdale branch. However, in 1879 optimism prevailed, and no expense seemed to be spared in the construction of stations on the northern line.

From St John's the first stone-built station was at a point where the line crossed the Peel-Ramsey road and emerged on to the cliff tops at St Germain's. (Nearer to St John's, a timber hut was provided in 1880 at a halt to serve the quarry at Poortown, subsequently named Peel Road.) St Germain's was intended to be the MNR's station for Peel, even though that town was some 2 miles away. The building featured the traditional double gables and tall chimneys, as seen on other MNR stations.

Owners have made assorted improvements and additions over the years, but it is still unmistakably a former MNR station. The public footpath passing in front of the station follows the course of the old line. Incidentally, the use of the apostrophe in St Germain's appears to have been disregarded by both the MNR and IMR, for it does not appear on any of the tickets issued from this station. Even at such an important station as St John's, the apostrophe was something of an optional extra – the MNR tickets did not use it at all, and on IMR issues it appears only intermittently. *Both EG*

The MNR line boasted two spectacular viaducts, both supported by massive stone pillars, to carry the line across first Glen Mooar, then, on the approach to Kirk Michael, Glen Wyllin, which No 12 *Hutchinson* is crossing with a two-coach Ramsey-Douglas train on the 5 July 1950. The village of Kirk Michael and its church tower may be seen in the distance. Below the viaduct, Glen Wyllin itself had been developed as a popular destination for both island residents and visitors, including a boating lake and facilities for assorted sports and pastimes. From 1935 it was owned by the IMR, and tickets to Kirk Michael often included admission to the glen.

Today, the glen is a pleasant camp site, and offers a splendid walk to the beach, but most of the other attractions have disappeared. Of the Glen Wyllin viaduct, as at Glen Mooar, after the girders were removed in 1975 only the stone pillars remain to remind us of what was once there. *Both EG*

Kirk Michael was the nearest station to the Glen Wyllin pleasure grounds, and as such attracted a good deal of seasonal traffic. The resemblance of the station building to those at St Germain's, Ballaugh and Sulby Bridge may be noted. A Ramsey-bound five-coach train in the charge of No 8 *Fenella* straddles the level crossing as it comes to a halt. The single-line staff is being handed to the driver, indicating that he has permission to proceed into the next section. On the south side of the crossing a water tower was situated at the end of the single-line length from St Germain's.

The station is now occupied by the Isle of Man Fire Service, the appliances being housed in the former goods shed, out of the picture to the left. *TT/EG*

Looking north at Kirk Michael on 30 May 1953, No 3 *Pender* has just arrived with the 12.35pm train from Ramsey, and the driver is taking the opportunity to walk round with his oil can. The goods shed may be seen beyond the station building, displaying an enamel advertising plaque for Petter Oil Engines. Similar plaques were to be seen on other Isle of Man stations, a source of supplementary revenue. The bunting adorning the station frontage was probably for the Coronation of Elizabeth II.

Today's view from the same angle, but taken from the other side of the road crossing, includes a short length of track and one crossing gate, reminders of how things once were. Embedded in the road surface to the left of the gate, another section of track, which once formed part of the original passing loop, is still visible. *HBP/EG*

From Kirk Michael, the next station on the line to Ramsey was Ballaugh, a similar structure. A new bungalow now covers the site of the station building, and little else remains, apart from a grass-covered platform, which was once alongside the cattle dock, and a goods shed. However, at Sulby Glen, seen here, the former station has been transformed into a pleasant dwelling house, retaining some of the original features. Sulby Glen was a popular destination for visitors, and was unusual in having a canopy over the platform. No 8 *Fenella*, for a long time the Ramsey-based engine, waits at the platform before resuming its journey.

The present-day view, taken from the rear of the building, includes a part of the crossing gate. One of the platform stanchions may be noted. *TT/EG*

Sulby Bridge station was a typical Manx Northern stone building with twin gables. Accommodation included a waiting hall, booking office, ladies' room and lamp room, while palm trees on the northern side of the track lent a tropical touch to the site. No 8 *Fenella* starts off with a Ramsey-bound train. The station once had a passing loop and a siding, both lifted by the time this picture was taken.

Today, the station building is an attractive private dwelling house. *TT/EG*

Above Ramsey was the headquarters of the Manx Northern Railway, and the station occupied an extensive site at the upper end of the harbour. In this 1947 view the carriage shed dominates the picture (centre), a rake of coaches stands at the platform, and a locomotive assembles stock in the bay platform (right). Tracks to the left of the carriage shed led to a cattle dock, goods shed, ore shed, coaling stack and water tower. The line on the extreme left, where an open wagon is parked, gave access to the harbourside extension. *RP*

Above No 3 *Pender* (now a 'sectioned' exhibit at the Manchester Museum of Science and Technology) is seen in 1953 against a backdrop of coaches at the main platform, and the inner side of the station offices. *HBP*

Right No 8 *Fenella* was photographed on 30 June 1965 by the coal stack. Note the weighbridge incorporated into the track. By the wall on the right is the track to the harbour tramway. *EG*

The façade of Ramsey station building and the administrative offices of the Manx Northern Railway faced southwards on to what was named, inevitably, Station Road (every town or village with a station seemed to have a Station Road!). The main platform was on the north side of the building, and the end of the platform awning may be seen on the extreme right.

Some ten years after the cessation of services the station building was demolished and the site cleared. The area once occupied by the railway has since been redeveloped as a mixed industrial estate, and the former site of the station building is now occupied by the Ramsey Bakery. *Both EG*

Above After the opening of its line from St John's to Ramsey in 1879 the MNR gained permission to extend the track from the terminus across Bowring Road and along the quayside to permit the discharge of coal direct from a ship into railway wagons – as the island had no natural supplies of coal, this was a principal import. The importance of this 1883 extension, known as the Harbour Tramway, was further increased when rail connection was made from St John's to the Foxdale lead mines in 1886. Thereafter, carriage of lead ore to Ramsey for shipment outwards, and inward traffic of coal, became the principal purpose of the harbour tramway. The IMR had made a similar application to extend its line on to the quayside at Douglas, but, despite the matter being raised frequently, this was never achieved, and the MNR gained an undoubted advantage. Its quayside line incorporated three short sidings off the main line, on which wagons could be left alongside the ship's berth. When filled, the wagons were assembled into a train for hauling along the quay to join the railway proper in the station precincts. Even when the export of ore ceased, imports of coal remained at a high level. The tramway and the first siding are seen on an otherwise deserted West Quay – the posts and chains could be removed to allow access. *TL*

Below Beyond the swing bridge were two more sidings. No 3 *Pender* is seen on the first of these, alongside the steamer berth, preparing to remove loaded wagons. *KH&SD*

The Harbour Tramway continued in use until 1948-49, when the last imports to be carried over the metals were a cargo of steel rails from Workington and two cargoes of coal for the railway's own use. The intermittent use of the tracks in post-war years had led to problems of obstruction by parked vehicles. The tramway was also being rendered redundant by the increasing use of the ubiquitous motor lorry to distribute coal to all parts of the island. Consequently the IMR agreed to surrender the lease, and the Harbour Board lifted the track in stages in the period 1955-57. The lines downstream of the swing bridge are seen in this 1948 view, but today all trace of the tramway has vanished. *V/EG*

Isle of Man Railway:
Douglas to Port Erin

Although the steam train services to Peel and Ramsey have long since gone, the IMR's 1874 line between Douglas and Port Erin survives, albeit merely as a seasonal tourist attraction. Although there have been proposals to upgrade the service to offer an alternative commuter route into the capital, and even talk of re-instating the Peel line, it seems highly unlikely that anything will come of these schemes.

Leaving Douglas on the first leg of the 15-mile run to Port Erin, the locomotives have to take a good run at the steep gradient of the Nunnery bank. The climb continues through White Hoe, crossing the roadway at Kewaigue by a stone-arched bridge. No 4 *Loch* is working hard at Kewaigue as it tackles the rise to the summit at Keristal on 29 May 1985.

Highway improvements at this spot have included the construction of a new bridge (2001) and a re-alignment of the roadway to avoid the limited headroom and restricted width imposed by the 1873 structure. No 13 *Kissack* hauls the 10.15am departure from Douglas over the new bridge on the 14 August 2006. The original bridge still carries the track across a section of the old roadway, and may be glimpsed behind the greenery to the left. *Both EG*

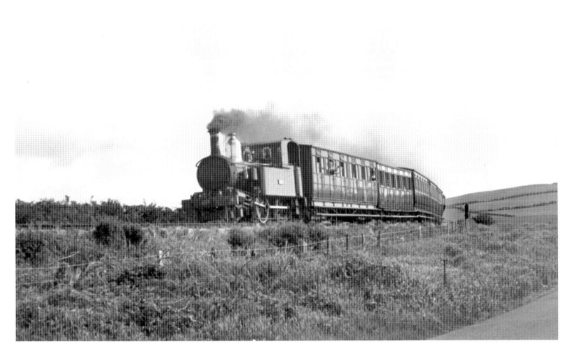

At Keristal summit, the line suddenly emerges from a cutting on to the cliff tops, where brief glimpses of the sea and the Marine Drive are offered before the line curves inland on the approach to Port Soderick station. No 4 *Loch* is easing off at the summit on a Port Erin-bound train in May 1985.

No 13 *Kissack* hauls a four-coach train at the same spot in September 2006. The field in the foreground was the scene of an amusing (for some) incident during one of the special transport events of the 1990s, when sheep grazing in the field were startled by the noise of a Beyer Peacock engine working hard and emitting a long blast on the whistle for the benefit of waiting photographers as it burst out of the cutting. The sheep stampeded and ran headlong into the waiting group, who had set up their equipment in readiness for the train to appear. Several photographs were spoiled that day! *Both EG*

Port Soderick station lies on a left-hand curve in a wooded setting. The station building is a substantial structure, dating from 1896, when it replaced an earlier timber building. Once an important halt for tourists spending an afternoon or evening at the Port Soderick beach amusements, it has known special trains of a dozen or so coaches needing two engines. Sadly, its use has diminished, reflecting the decline of Port Soderick itself, which is now practically deserted. The station building, which had lain out of use for some years, was sold in 1984, with a proviso that the buyer should not be allowed to alter the character of the structure, the IMR agreeing to erect a fence along the frontage to separate waiting passengers from the private house. No 10 *G. H. Wood* heads a train from some 20 years ago.

No 8 *Fenella* comes to a stand at the same spot on 14 August 2006. *Fenella* was a rare visitor to the south line in earlier years, the small-boilered engines being used mainly on the lighter trains to Peel and Ramsey. Both engines carry the usual collection of kettles and oil-cans on the front buffer beam. Until 2003 Port Soderick had one platform only, on the southbound side. A new northbound platform (left) now extends from the loop points to the boundary of the former station building. *Both EG*

Beyond Port Soderick the line passes through the Crogga woods before arriving at Santon. No 12 *Hutchinson* hauls a train of coaches in the purple lake and white livery that was used for a period in the 1980s and '90s.

A programme of repainting the carriage stock into the more popular and traditional livery of red and cream was begun in 2000-01. No 13 *Kissack* is seen approaching Santon on 23 September 2006. *Both EG*

Santon station is seen from the Castletown road bridge on 25 May 1981. The timber building was acquired in 1875 and a loop for passing trains was installed soon afterwards. The siding for the cattle dock may be noted on the right. As was usual for many IMR stations, no platforms were provided. At the time of the first photograph, only the northern side of the loop (left) was in use. A train from Douglas is arriving, and, surprisingly, for the halt was little used by the locals, there is one lady passenger (complete with umbrella) waiting to board.

The view from the same vantage point on 16 September 2006 shows several differences. The trackwork looks much more respectable, and the station has gained half-height platforms, constructed in the winter of 1999-2000. In the peak-period summer season of 2000 trains crossed at Santon and Castletown. *Both EG*

No 12 *Hutchinson* pulls into Santon on 14 August 1985, passing beneath the bridge that formed the vantage point for the two previous photographs. A second locomotive is banking the train at the rear. A group of open wagons stands on the former cattle dock siding (left), now in use for permanent way materials.

The transformation is complete in the picture of 23 September 2006, as No 4 *Loch* arrives to pick up passengers for Douglas. This time, only the south side of the loop is in use for trains in both directions. The railway gained a major bonus from the island's drainage scheme of 2001-03, which necessitated the laying of pipework beneath the trackbed, resulting in most of the Port Erin line being completely renewed. While work was in progress in the 2002 season the section between Santon and Castletown was closed, and Santon became the temporary northern terminus, from where passengers were conveyed onwards by coach. *Both EG*

As at Santon, the station building at Ballasalla was the customary IMR timber structure with corrugated-iron roof, and there were no platforms. Sited approximately at the halfway point of the south line, Ballasalla became, and remains, a regular crossing point for trains. In the 'past' picture a four-coach train from Douglas waits for the arrival of the train from Port Erin. The siding for the goods shed and cattle dock may be noted beyond the station building. In 1984 the northern portion of the station site (left), including the siding and cattle dock area, was sold to a developer who, in exchange for access to the car park, agreed to provide a replacement station building, but on the other side of the line. This was duly done, complete with platform, and opened with due ceremony in April 1986.

Fifteen years later a full-height platform has been provided alongside the Douglas-bound line, and the Port Erin line platform has been extended. The Douglas platform has merely a bus-type shelter for waiting passengers. No 13 *Kissack* waits with a southbound train for the Douglas train to arrive on 12 August 2006. *TT/EG*

From the other side of the tracks, this 1950s view of No 12 *Hutchinson* at the Port Erin platform at Ballasalla offers another view of the original station building. A goods van sits on the siding, and a porter with a trolley gazes down the track for a sight of the approaching Douglas train. The lack of platforms explains the necessity of footboards on the carriages.

The 1986 station building and the extended platform are apparent in the view of trains crossing on 23 September 2006. No 4 *Loch* waits alongside the Douglas-bound train, ready to depart for Port Erin. It is about to negotiate the busiest level crossing on the island, for at the west end of the station is the main road leading to the airport. *CCT/EG*

Castletown, the former capital of the island, is the busiest intermediate station on the line, reflected in the animated scenes of both illustrations. The station building was unusual for the IMR, in that it was a stone-built twin-gable structure, with a veranda. As usual there were no platforms. On 27 May 1985 No 12 *Hutchinson*, then in its rebuilt form and sporting blue livery, is hauling a well-patronised train to Port Erin, while in the background the ex-County Donegal railcars are waiting for a special party. The railcars were relatively rare visitors to Castletown: they had been tested and found wanting on the gradient of the Nunnery bank, where fallen leaves tended to cause wheel slip because of lack of adhesive weight. They performed more satisfactorily on the Peel line, which became their more usual sphere of operations.

Half-height platforms were installed in the late 1990s, and the station subsequently benefited from the pipeline-relaying project and today presents a much more acceptable face of the railway. The driver of No 4 *Loch* receives the single-line staff on 16 September 2006. *Both EG*

The northern side of a platform-less loop at Castletown is the location of this view of No 10 *G. H. Wood* as veteran driver John Elkin takes the opportunity to oil a few moving parts as he waits to depart with a train of four purple lake and white coaches. John Elkin was driver of one of the last locomotives to negotiate the Ramsey line in 1968. His fireman, Jeffrey Kelly (later to become a well-known driver on the south line), recalled that after the last trip on the Ramsey line he was sent back to set fire to the remains of a van body that had served as a store shed at the Peel Road (Poortown) station.

The start of the operating season on 2 April 2007 saw locomotives Nos 4 and 8 in use, each making two return trips per day. No 8 *Fenella* was the Port Erin-based engine. Traffic being light, the trains were made up of only three coaches. The half-height platforms, new fencing and new track are the main differences in this view of the 14.10 Douglas-bound service from Port Erin. *Both EG*

The site of Ballabeg Halt, which lay some distance from Ballabeg village, was marked only by a platelayers' hut in post-war years. Trains stopped not at all, or occasionally on request. The 'past' view was taken on 29 June 1972 looking westwards towards Port Erin and the bridge carrying the Arbory to Castletown road.

A small veranda was added to the platelayers' hut in 1987, and subsequently a platform and signboard appeared, restoring the charm to this little-used halt. The platform was lengthened and raised slightly in 2004, and can now accommodate four coaches. The new trackwork is in evidence in this September 2006 view. *Both EG*

The original layout at Colby was similar to that at Ballasalla – a wooden building, platform-less station, and a cattle dock siding at the eastern end. Level crossings were provided at both ends of the station, but these were little used, giving access only to agricultural land. The 'past' view, looking eastwards on 28 June 1972, gives some idea of the rather neglected air that hung about the place.

Contrast the present-day view, with new signboard, a smartly painted shelter (ex-Braddan), re-laid track, and full-height generously long platforms on both sides, constructed during the relay of 2004. No 4 *Loch* arrives at the head of a Port Erin train on 16 September 2006. The northern loop is currently used for trains in both directions. *Both EG*

Colby Level lies a little further westwards along the track from Colby itself. There was little here except the gate-keeper's hut (left), but trains would stop if the driver had been so advised by the guard. If passengers were waiting to board, the gate-keeper would display a red flag. Photographed in 1972, the crossing appears neglected, with vegetation rampant and untrimmed.

During the winter of 1999-2000 a short raised platform was constructed in front of the crossing-keeper's hut, extending for approximately the length of one coach. The crossing now has the usual automated barriers, and a smart sign on the fence bears the title 'THE LEVEL', while above the window, by the platform bench, is painted 'COLBY LEVEL CROSSING'. It is usually referred to merely as 'Level'. Seen here on 14 August 2006, is this the smallest station in the British Isles? *Both EG*

The survival of the Port Erin line as a seasonal tourist attraction was because it offered greater revenue-earning potential than the Peel or Ramsey lines, and there were likely to be fewer operational problems. Except for the busy road at Ballasalla, the level crossings were mainly confined in the south to minor roads, as here at Ballagawne. The crossing-keeper here was once an elderly lady, who arrived by bicycle when trains were due, opened the gates when she heard the engine whistling in the distance at Colby Level, and waved the appropriate flag to indicate to the driver that all was well and he could proceed. In between trains, she went home or tidied the garden by the hut. On cold days, enginemen would throw out lumps of coal for her fire.

Today the gate-keepers' huts are deserted, and crossings are guarded by automated barriers, complete with audible warnings, which are activated on the approach of the train. No 13 *Kissack* approaches on 7 September 2006. *Both EG*

Port St Mary has but a single platform, and lacks a passing loop, but boasts the largest, most imposing station building outside Douglas, reflecting its former status as one of the busiest spots on the line. The red-brick structure dates from 1898, when it replaced an earlier timber building. No 10 *G. H. Wood*, on a Douglas-bound train, will have left the Port Erin terminus only 4 minutes earlier.

No 4 *Loch* stands at the same spot on 3 September 2006. The station building was last fully utilised by the railway in the mid-1970s, since when it has been leased for a variety of purposes, including a Youth Hostel, the Station Master being relegated to a small hut on the platform. There is a scheme under consideration that would restore the booking office and waiting room for railway use, while the rest of the building would be converted into apartments. *Both EG*

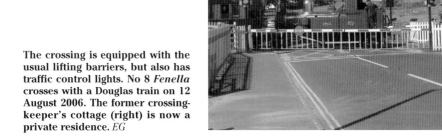

The crossing is equipped with the usual lifting barriers, but also has traffic control lights. No 8 *Fenella* crosses with a Douglas train on 12 August 2006. The former crossing-keeper's cottage (right) is now a private residence. *EG*

At the western end of Port St Mary station on 6 May 1995 No 10 *G. H. Wood* pulls away with a four-coach Port Erin train in the purple lake and white livery.

Little has changed here except the livery in this 9 September 2006 view of No 12 *Hutchinson* at the same location. The locomotive is in Indian red, the carriages in red and cream. After its 1980 rebuild with the larger cab, *Hutchinson* was returned to more traditional appearance and lost its blue livery during a major overhaul in 1999-2000. The former goods shed and cattle dock siding are to the right. *Both EG*

The end of the line is reached at Port Erin, 15½ miles from Douglas. The station building was erected in 1903 to replace the original. One of the railway motor lorries is occupying the platform in this view from September 1956, while a rake of coaches occupies the bay platform.

The former bay platform roads were lifted in 1975 and the area altered to provide parking spaces for buses. The bus garage (behind the photographer) was converted into a railway museum and houses a collection of interesting exhibits, large and small, ranging from complete locomotives to tickets. A new carriage shed to accommodate ten coaches was constructed in 1998 at the eastern end of the station. On 12 August 2006 No 8 *Fenella* had just left her train and moved to the buffer stop prior to reversing on the release road. On the current

timetable 57 minutes are allowed for the journey from Douglas – it used to be 50, and in pre-war days 40 for the non-stop expresses. Between trains, locomotives are coaled and watered at a stone-built engine shed (off the picture to the right). *CCT/EG*

Douglas Street Tramways, horse-drawn and cable

Victoria Pier and Arcade, Douglas, I.O.M.

After the opening of the railway to Port Erin in 1874, the next railed transport to appear in the island was 'The Douglas Bay Tramway'. Intending to profit from the island's popularity with Victorian holidaymakers, Thomas Lightfoot opened the first section of his tramway along the Douglas promenade in 1876, using three horse-drawn tramcars. As with the steam railway, a gauge of 3 feet was chosen. After sale in 1882 to the Isle of Man Tramways Limited, an extension was made to Derby Castle at the north end of the promenade. In this 1913 view several 'toast-rack' (cross-bench) tramcars, together with many horse-drawn carriages, are visible on the pier, all waiting to transport arriving passengers to their boarding houses and hotels. A sign of things to come is the single motor car.

The last horse-drawn tramway in the British Isles survives today, operated by Douglas Corporation as a seasonal tourist attraction. Trams no longer terminate on the pier, although a section of track remains. The sea terminal has been rebuilt and private cars have taken the place of the cabs and carriages. Covered 'toast-rack' 35, supplied originally by the Birkenhead firm of G. F. Milnes in 1896, stands at the present terminus opposite the end of Victoria Street. *V/EG*

Although the view towards the pier and sea terminal has changed considerably, the prospect inland includes many recognisable buildings. Car 45, a 1907 product of the United Electric Car Company of Preston, has reached the terminus on 28 May 1986 and the horse is about to be unhitched before being attached to the other end of the car. The sea terminal is to the left, and Victoria Street leads off to the right. The Bay Tramway fares were twopence in summer, one penny in winter.

The shops in the background have changed occupants and uses over the years, and what was once the Grand Hotel (to the right of the tramcar) is now occupied by the Anglo-Irish Bank and the offices of an insurance company. Car 35 is on duty on 7 September 2006. *Both EG*

From a vantage point at an upper window of the building seen in the two previous illustrations, the photographer is looking northwards along Loch Promenade. The clock at the end of Victoria Street, erected in 1887 in celebration of Queen Victoria's Jubilee, is prominent. The wide sweep of the bay – the full route of the horse tramway – is to be noted. Crossbench car 35 appears again, but in original form, without the glazed bulkheads that it gained only in 1966-67. Ahead of it is open 'toast-rack' 40, new from G. F. Milnes in 1902.

From much the same vantage point, but at ground level, today's view of the arc of Victorian hotels and boarding houses seems much the same, except that motor cars have crept into the view. Many of the former hotels have now been converted into apartments, for the tourist trade is not what it was. Car 33, another Milnes product of 1896, is about to use the crossover to start its journey along the promenade. *Commercial postcard/EG*

Derby Castle terminus, at the north end of the Douglas promenade, became the starting point for the electric tramway in 1893, and both horse and electric cars are seen in this pre-1896 postcard view. An open 'toast-rack' car is ready to return southwards, and an electric car waits for northbound passengers. In 1896 an ornate canopy was erected to cover the four terminal tracks of the horse tramway, thereby providing shelter for waiting passengers on both systems. The building on the left survives today as the Terminus Tavern.

Only three horse-tram tracks form the present terminus of the horse tramway, seen here on 24 September 2006, and the great canopy was demolished in 1980. The horse tram depot is off the picture to the left, alongside the Terminus Tavern, reached by tracks branching off in the foreground. In the operating season the cars in use are stored outside for convenience on the track ends. The Terminus Tavern does a good trade in lunchtime meals – diners are able to sit in the sunshine and watch operations on the two tramways. *Commercial postcard/EG*

By 1894 the horse-drawn tramway had been acquired by the company constructing the electric tramway to Laxey. The purchase had as its objective the eventual upgrading and the running of electric cars all the way along the promenade to the steamer berths on the Victoria Pier, but as part of the bargain the new owners were obliged to build a tramway to serve Upper Douglas. Hoteliers and retailers in areas away from the seafront claimed that boarding houses and shops in the upper parts of the town were placed at a disadvantage, and there was a demand for public transport to serve their districts. In view of the gradients involved, a tramway would have to use mechanical power, so in 1896 the Upper Douglas Cable Tramway began operation, constructed by the Isle of Man Tramways Company, owner of the horse and

electric tramways. The chosen gauge was again 3 feet, and there was a connection to the horse-tram lines. Sadly, after the failure of Dumbell's Bank in 1900, and having underestimated the cost of extending the electric line to Ramsey, the company became bankrupt. Douglas Corporation purchased both horse and cable tramways in 1902 for the sum of £50,000.

The cable tramway started at a point near the Victoria clock, a favourite viewpoint for postcard photographers. On the left an open-ended cable car of the 79-82 series (cable car numbers at first began at 71 so as not to conflict with any possible increase in the 37-strong horse-tram fleet) stands at the terminus, ready to commence the climb up Victoria Street. As on the San Francisco system, the cars were powered by a continuously moving cable under the tracks. The driver operated a gripping mechanism through a slot between the lines, by which he could hold or release the cable.

In recent times, during road repairs at this point, workmen uncovered the remains of the pit holding the large pulley around which the cable ran at the terminus. The site is now marked by a section of cable tram track, though the centre slot has been filled for safety reasons. *Commercial postcard/EG*

VICTORIA STREET, DOUGLAS.

Opposite page The terminus of the cable car route is seen here looking up Victoria Street, showing the connection to the horse tram tracks in the left foreground. The horse-drawn tramway was extended to the steamer berths under Douglas Corporation ownership, and at one time there was a shuttle service of trams bringing passengers from the pier to the cable car terminus. The 2-mile route began here, and passed along Victoria Street and the steep gradients of Prospect Hill and Bucks Road to reach Woodbourne Road.

Victoria Street is now one-way only, and direct access from the promenade is blocked; flower tubs cover the spot where the track was exposed. The new building behind the Victoria Clock is the Royal Bank of Scotland, built on the site of the old Villiers Hotel. The former Grand Hotel, now the offices of the Anglo-Irish Bank and Tower Insurance, is on the left. *Commercial postcard/EG*

This page Cable car 72, lightly loaded, climbs a steep portion of Prospect Hill as it passes Dumbell's Bank in 1896. To be carried to the higher parts of the town cost the traveller twopence, but the ride downwards cost only one penny. Tired holidaymakers returning to their boarding houses in Upper Douglas thought the higher fare well worthwhile; even so, the cable tramway operated at a loss.

Buildings seen in the earlier view survive today. The imposing structure on the left is now the HSBC bank. 10 September 2006. *SRK/EG*

At Avondale corner on Woodbourne Road, opposite the newly built Newsome Terrace, the cable tramway reached its highest point. Beyond was open country, which the promoters correctly forecast would soon become populated. Cable car No 73 may have been on a short working about 1896, ready to return along the busiest section of the line to the Jubilee Clock, for beyond was the acute right turn into York Road and the descent to Broadway, which proved troublesome in operation.

The terrace is still recognisable on 10 September 2006, but the rest of the scene has changed, and subsequent housing development now extends to cover the open countryside in the former view. *Commercial postcard/EG*

The tramway depot and winding house were located on York Road, on the descent via Ballaquayle Road to the Broadway terminus, close to the promenade, where a projected junction with the horse-tram line did not materialise. In fact, difficulties in working this section led to the Broadway length being abandoned as early as 1901. Drifting sand from the beach clogged the cable conduit slot on the lower section, and the wheel pit became flooded at certain high tides. The narrowness of the street and the gradients involved added to the difficulties, and led to the terminus being moved some distance uphill to a kerbside location at Stanley Terrace on Ballaquayle Road, where car 82 waits for passengers in about 1902.

Stanley Terrace remains, photographed on 10 September 2006, and not far away on Waverley Road a short length of track is visible; under Corporation ownership, the horse trams were repaired and maintained at the York Road Depot, being transferred to the cable tramway at the Jubilee Clock and hauled thence by cable car, and this was a piece of the track over which the horse trams were once towed into the winter storage shed. *RH/EG*

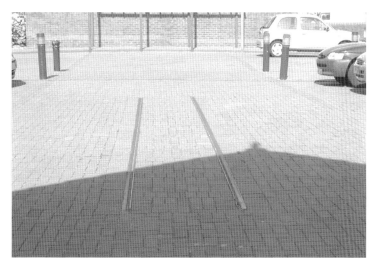

The cable tramway ceased operation in 1929. Douglas Corporation had purchased motor buses as early as 1920, and from 1921 the cable cars had been worked as a seasonal service, latterly running mainly in July and August only. The 16 cars were sold off to a dealer who intended to convert them to holiday bungalows, though the two pictured here (No 80 nearest the camera) appear to have been allocated for another use.

Cars 72 and 73 survived as bungalows in the north of the island until 1968, when they were acquired for preservation and restoration. Using parts from both cars, Keith Pearson and team have reconstructed 72-73 as one vehicle, which is now stored in the horse tram depot at Derby Castle. *ADP/EG*

The Manx Electric Railway and the Laxey Mines Railway

The Manx Electric Railway began operation as far as Groudle in 1893, once again with a track gauge of 3 feet. The line was extended in stages to its full length of more than 17¾ miles, reaching Ramsey in 1899. Alas, the aim to serve the full length of the promenade to the sea terminal was not, and still has not, been achieved, costing the MER many millions of passengers over the years. In this 1904 view, Edwardian holidaymakers crowd the Derby Castle terminus as a line of tramcars waits to carry passengers northwards. The horse-tram depot appears on the extreme left, the great canopy may be noted (centre), and the Derby Castle amusement complex (right).

Today the crowds have vanished, together with the great canopy and the Derby Castle complex. The hotel and the horse-tram depot and terminus remain (partly hidden by the bus-type shelter) as tramcar 22 waits to commence its journey on 8 August 2006. Car 5 with trailer waits to take its place on the terminal stub. Between the two electric cars may be seen some horse-trams, stored on the end of their line. The electric tram depot may be noted below the sign, far right. *Commercial postcard/EG*

Car 20 stands with trailer and goods van on the terminal stub at Derby Castle on 26 June 1965. The rustic-style booking office was constructed in 1897 between the tracks of the electric and horse-drawn tramways. Note the sacks outside the booking office, and the weighing machine, which stood at its corner for many years. Until 1975 the tramway had the contract to empty the post-boxes along the route, and also carried goods and parcels.

Car 21 stands on the same spot on 7 June 2006. The four closed cars numbered 19-22 were supplied new by the G. F. Milnes Company in 1899. They are the largest cars on the system, and have a seating capacity of 48. The 'winter saloons', as they are known, have formed the backbone of the fleet in both winter and summer ever since their arrival, and continue to do so today. A concession to modernity is that since 1932 they have had upholstered seats. The 1897 booking office remains in use – one well-known motorman, the late A. M. Goodwyn, used to refer to it as 'our downtown booking facility'. *Both EG*

From a vantage point a few yards further up the track, the Derby Castle terminus booking office is hidden by two goods vans parked on the siding, close to the canopy over the horse-tram tracks. Car 5 has just arrived and been detached from trailer 41.

Trailer 41 is seen again, this time coupled to car 21, having just arrived at Derby Castle on 7 June 2006, and the reversing procedure is about to begin. The demolition of the canopy has allowed the Terminus Tavern (right) and the horse tram depot to come into view. The upper storey above the horse-tram shed was a later addition, which became the head office of Isle of Man Transport until the present Lakes Road (Banks Circus) premises were completed in 2000. Today the former offices are available for hire as a banqueting suite. *Both EG*

Looking northwards at Derby Castle, the Victorian photographer has captured the scene before the turn of the 20th century, when the company title was 'Douglas & Laxey Coast Electric Tramway'. A tramcar of the 4-9 series, supplied new in 1894 for the extension to Laxey, is about to haul well-loaded trailer 15. The presence of the police constables suggests that this may have been a special occasion, or a trial run. In their early years the first electric cars drew current from the overhead wires by means of bow collectors, which proved troublesome and were later replaced by trolley poles.

Car 7 of the same series (sometimes known as 'tunnel cars' because of their interior layout) reverses on the crossover on 29 June 1965. The castellated wall of Derby Castle, constructed in 1894, began at the entrance gates (off the picture to the left) and ran parallel with the track. Car 7 appears in a much less ornate 'economy' livery, the company title being abbreviated merely to 'M.E.R'.

In June 1984, the date of the third picture, the Derby Castle entertainment centre has gone and the area behind the tram has become a car park for a new leisure complex. The ill-fated 'Summerland' was re-born after the disastrous fire of 1973 as the 'Aquadrome', alongside which trailer 41 waits as the conductor of car 6 places the trolley neatly on the overhead wire prior to the car moving to the parallel track. The procedure for changing ends at termini is for the power car to uncouple and reverse over the crossover to the adjoining track while the conductor releases the brake on the trailer and allows it to roll down by gravity. The power car then reverses again and couples to the upper end ready to leave on the next journey. Similar movements may be observed at Laxey and Ramsey. Note that at this date the title of the undertaking appeared as 'Isle of Man Passenger Transport'.

Finally we see that the view northwards from the booking office and terminal stub is greatly changed today. The demolition of the ugly 'Aquadrome' was completed in 2006, and a decision on the future of the site has yet to be reached. Winter saloon 21 has just arrived from Ramsey and is about to detach from its trailer. Note the 'clock' with its representation of a 4-9 series tramcar, advising passengers of the departure time of the next car. *M&P/EG (3)*

A short distance north of the terminus lies the Derby Castle Depot and Works. In the 1894 view the original boiler house is behind the tall chimney, with the engine house beyond. The barn-like building is the No 1 Car Shed of 1893. Tracks in the foreground, on which a trailer is parked, led to the second car shed. The boiler house and engine house were converted to become a goods shed (1908) and machine shop (1904) respectively, after a new generating system was brought into use and Derby Castle became merely a sub-station.

The second picture shows the lower shed area in 1961. The boiler house was replaced by a pitched-roof car shed (No 6) in 1923, while the higher roof of the original engine house remains visible behind. The end of the

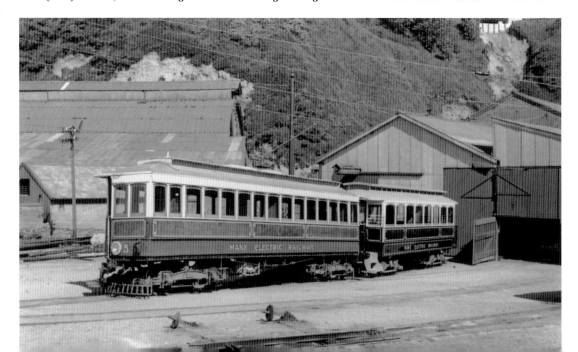

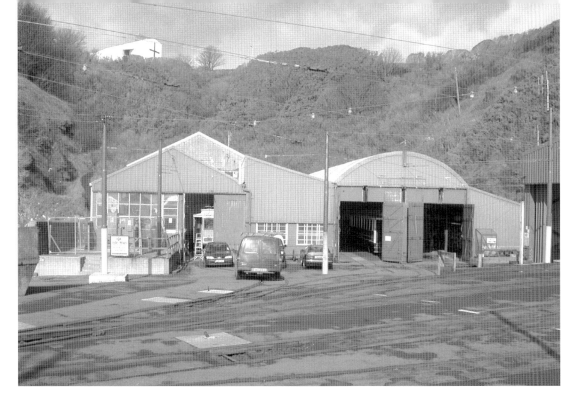

original Derby Castle amusement complex may be noted in both illustrations. Car 5 is coupled to one of the two winter saloon trailers, Nos 57 and 58, purchased in 1903. Now rarely used, the corner entrance steps allowed the conductor to move between vehicles; Health & Safety inspectors do not now approve of such arrangements, and conductors are forbidden to move on the open footboards of trailers when cars are in motion.

The lower part of the depot complex is seen today in the third view, with No 6 car shed in use as the joiners' shop and paint shop. The three-road No 1 shed has the stores alongside, and the end of the new upper sheds, constructed in 1996-97 to replace the life-expired and inadequate buildings that grew up piecemeal in the 1894-96 period, is just visible on the extreme right.

The demolition of the 'Aquadrome' now permits an uninterrupted view of the depot area, as seen in the final picture, from July 2006. The original engine house is clearly seen on the extreme left, and the replacement top sheds on the right. There were no fewer than 13 tracks within the depot complex, and the laying of a new fan of lines to serve the new sheds caused problems in 1997-99. Operational difficulties were caused by severe curves and restricted clearances, and the trackwork had to be completely re-laid in consequence. The 'Electric Railway' illuminated sign retains its prominent position above the depot. A new apartment block rises on the cliff top, offering an unrivalled view of operations in the depot yard. *M&P/ADP/EG (2)*

The view of Derby Castle Depot yard from above in 1972 shows the old car sheds and track layout as it used to be. Crossbench car 27 and two goods vans stand in front of the No 6 lower shed, and a car of the 4-9 series is parked at the seaward side. The rear edge of the 'Summerland' leisure centre appears top right. By the entrance to the depot yard, where the track branches inwards from the main running line, the small hut (built 1924) serves as the office of the Depot Foreman, where crews sign on at the beginning of their shift.

The scene from above today is quite different. The absence of the leisure complex offers an unrestricted view southwards towards the terminus and along the promenade, and immediately below are the roofs of the new depot. On completion of duty, the motorman records details of his journeys and reports any faults in the hut of the Depot Foreman, which survives unchanged. *Both EG*

In Derby Castle Depot yard on 28 May 1985 two of the six cars of the 4-9 series of 1894, of which four remain, are in view (cars 4 and 8 were lost in 1930 in a fire at Laxey Depot). Car 9, then appearing in an 'historic livery' and bearing the company title as the 'Douglas Laxey & Ramsey Electric Railway', is propelling its trailer into the middle road of the lower shed, while car 5 sits on a siding by the upper shed. This latter siding was removed in 1988.

In the Depot yard on 19 July 1997 the new sheds are in evidence, but trackwork for the upper sheds has not yet been completed. Many vehicles had to be stored in the open while this work was progressing. Winter saloon 19, then finished in another 'historic livery', the 1899-style of cream and brown, stands amid the debris, while car 7 has just emerged from the 'hospital road' of No 1 shed, so-called because that is the track for minor repairs and adjustments. *Both EG*

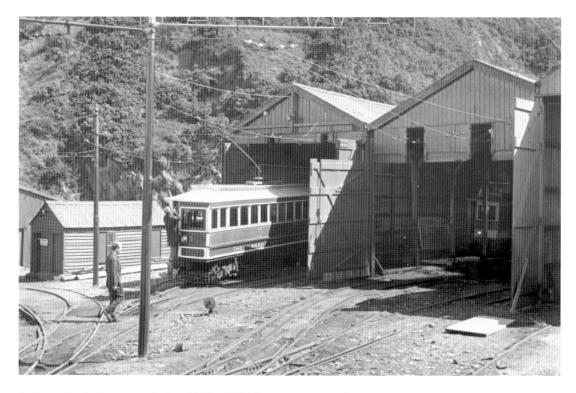

At Derby Castle Depot top shed on 28 May 1985 the conductor carefully guides the trolley head on the intricate overhead wiring as car 5 is carefully driven into No 8 track of the top shed. Note the company title on the side panel as 'The Manx Electric Railway'. The depot site slopes downwards away from the entrance, and consequently tracks in the original upper sheds were not always at the same level. The presence of inspection pits between the rails in this dimly lit area was a hazard for the unwary.

When the problems of the track fan had been resolved, eight of the nine tracks into the new top shed were on the level and accessible. However, the ninth road, at a lower level, intended to serve a small workshop area, had a sharp descending right-hand curve, making access difficult. This has since been disconnected. Crossbench cars 31 and 26 stand in the sunshine on 8 August 2002. Car 31 was one of four cars (28-31) supplied by the United Electric Car Company of Preston in 1904, ordered to meet growing traffic demands. It is one of the two remaining serviceable cars not fitted with an air-braking system, relying on the ratchet only. Though thoroughly refurbished in 1993, car 31 is rarely seen outside the depot. Car 26 was originally a trailer, one of four dating from 1899 that were converted to power cars in 1903 by the fitting of new trucks, traction motors and electrical equipment. The upgrading required alterations to the footboards to clear the axle-boxes, the resulting uneven line of the footboard earning the name 'paddlebox' for these cars – compare with the straight footboard on car 31. The Z-shaped-bar lying on the left footboard of 26 is a connecting bar for a trailer. *Both EG*

From Derby Castle Depot entrance, the main line climbs northwards, running parallel with the roadway. The proximity of road and rail is no accident, as the original powers gained from Tynwald in 1892 were to develop part of the Howstrake Estates by constructing both road and railway from the north end of the promenade via Port Jack to Groudle. Car 9, in its 1899-style 'Douglas Laxey & Ramsey Electric Railway' livery, is nearing the end of its journey from Ramsey as it approaches the depot entrance on the descent from Port Jack in 1985.

Cars 1 and 2 of 1893 are the oldest electric tramcars still operating on their original line anywhere in the world. Car 1 is in the depot yard as car 2, displaying yet another variation of historic livery, passes by on 21 June 2004. The 'Douglas & Laxey Coast Electric Tramway' was the earliest title used by the company. The blue dash-plate of 2002 was a short-lived variation of the more usual dark maroon livery of these two cars, possibly an attempt to recreate what may have been the original Prussian blue of its earliest days; it has now reverted to maroon. The starboard list of the Douglas-end dash plate is evidently not alarming the driver. *Both EG*

The row of shops on the curve at Port Jack, seen here looking south, has changed but little in the last 50 years, and the old flight of concrete steps that once led up to the Douglas Bay Hotel continues to provide a good vantage point for photographers. Car 6 crosses the junction of King Edward Road and Harbour Road, Onchan, in the early 1950s. Note the split windscreen for the driver, and the dirty roof, the latter caused by fine copper deposits disturbed by the trolley as it passes along the overhead wire.

Car 7 is seen at the same spot many years later. The platform end windows were altered on these cars in 1966-68, when one-piece windscreens were fitted to improve forward visibility for the driver. In 1969 car 5 became the first in the fleet to have an electrically operated windscreen wiper. *RFM/EG*

Viewed from the opposite side of the road, the curve at Port Jack is seen again in 1960, as a 'tunnel car' of the 5-9 series hauls trailer 59 towards Douglas. Trailer 59 is the smallest passenger vehicle on the MER, seating only 18. Originally purchased to act as the Directors' Saloon, it was delivered in 1895 with superior fitments, and became known as the 'Royal Saloon' after carrying King Edward VII and Queen Alexandra in 1902. It is sometimes used for small private parties or special events, but otherwise sees little service.

The overhead line crew attend to a faulty bracket arm at the same spot in August 2002. Car 7, propelling the tower wagon, was at that time allocated to serve as the Poles & Wires works vehicle, and was in far from pristine condition. Watching progress from the roadway, in high-visibility jacket, is the then Director of Transport, David Howard, for, embarrassingly, the failure had occurred during a weekend of special events for transport enthusiasts. *ADP/EG*

Above Onchan Head, a short distance north of Douglas promenade, was once the site of a popular amusement park, and as such enjoyed a frequent shuttle service of cars to and from Derby Castle. Because the track at the White City Funfair had only a single crossover, the short service was usually provided by a crossbench car working without a trailer. Ratchet car 17 returns to Douglas with the expanse of the park on the seaward side. *RFM*

Middle and bottom The pleasure park closed in 1985, and the shuttle service is no more, both vanishing as housing estates spread northwards from the town centre. Onchan Head boasted its own stop sign when 'tunnel car' 7 passed on the Ramsey-Douglas service. Note the car livery, with careful lining-out of the panels and the full company title supplemented with 'M.E.R' above.

Today the site of the pleasure park is occupied by a new housing development, and the gardens of modern bungalows edge the tram track. Crossbench car 32, one of the two most 'modern' cars in the fleet (new in 1906), approaches the bus-type shelter at Onchan on 27 July 2006. *RFM/EG*

The line continues to climb parallel to the former toll road towards Howstrake. As it swings around the bend at Far End, the sweep of Douglas Bay can be seen to the south. Car 5 and trailer take the curve in the 1950s.

An unchanged vista forms the backdrop in 1995 as well-loaded car 7, newly out of the paint shop, hauls trailer 56. The latter was rebuilt from its original 1904 form to be an 'accessibility trailer', able to accommodate wheelchairs by means of a hoist. The conductor defies the Health & Safety Inspectors by riding on the footboard. *RFM/EG*

Car 3 and trailer 15 are on a test run in August 1893. The first three cars were equipped with Dr John Hopkinson's patent bow collectors, which, despite modifications, continued to cause trouble until replaced by the proven trolley wheel system in 1898. The first three cars accommodated 38 on longitudinal seats. Six trailers, each seating 44, had been ordered at the same time, in the vain hope that each power car would be able to haul two trailers. In the background is Groudle Bay; the Howstrake Holiday Camp once faced across the bay at this point.

The road has been surfaced, but the general view on 20 July 1997 remains largely unchanged. From this point in summer one may see trains on the restored Groudle Glen Miniature Railway as they travel to the headland. Winter saloon 22 was badly damaged by fire in 1990, but the car body was reconstructed in superb fashion, and the car re-entered service in 1992, complete with a public address system, electric bells, and other improvements. *M&P/EG*

At Half Way House the tramway meets and crosses the main Douglas to Laxey road and runs alongside it to Baldrine. Southbound winter saloon 21 leaves the Baldrine halt in July 1967, unusually, for the summer season, running without a trailer.

On 10 August 2002 car 21 is heading northwards at the same spot, hauling the small trailer 59, the former Directors' Saloon, on a special working to Ramsey. *ADP/EG*

The passenger shelter at Baldrine dates from 1899, and was renovated in 1991-92. It still possess a Royal Mail letter box on the north side of the hut, though the mail is no longer collected by MER conductors acting as auxiliary postmen. The motorman on the crossbench car on this occasion is the late A. M. Goodwyn, Chairman of the Manx Electric Railway Society. Car 24 was one of those destroyed in the Laxey Depot fire of 1930, and this '24' was really 26 in temporary disguise during a transport enthusiasts' event.

The postbox and shelter are seen again from the minor road to the north as car 5 crosses cautiously on 8 June 2006. The crossing was the scene of an unfortunate accident in 2003 when winter saloon 20 and a milk tanker collided, leaving the tram out of service for some considerable time. Another variation of the standard livery sees car 5 carrying the company title in Manx Gaelic – historically incorrect, but perhaps approved for the same reason as the use of some dual-language route information on the electronic destination indicators of the buses. Visitors to the island must be mystified, if not confused, to encounter a bus whose main destination reads 'Doolish' or, even worse, 'Rhumsaa', apparently displayed at the whim of the driver. Who buys a ticket to Rhumsaa when they travel to Ramsey? *Both EG*

Fairy Cottage is an intriguing name for this halt on the descent to Laxey. The weed-covered track of the Fairy Cottage crossover and the dilapidated shelter are apparent in this view of 6 July 1982 as car 22 with trailer 40 draws to a halt.

The weeds have been cleared in the later view, and the shelter has gained a clearer signboard, but otherwise the view is unchanged. Cars 18 and 31 are the only serviceable ratchet (ie non-air-brake) cars remaining in the fleet; others are 'in store', but unusable, robbed of vital components. Car 18 is rarely used, and on this occasion was towing van No 4 with motorman Miles Corlett at the controls for a demonstration run. *ADP/EG*

South Cape is the halt for those passengers wishing to visit the harbour at Old Laxey, and a sign advises passengers to alight here for the beach. Douglas-bound winter saloon 19 comes to a halt to pick up waiting passengers in July 1960.

In the more recent view the sign has been amended to include the advice 'Keep Your Seats For Laxey & Snaefell', which is correct only for northbound passengers; those travelling south will have already passed the stop for Laxey and Snaefell. Rebuilt car 22 passes South Cape in August 1995. *ADP/EG*

From South Cape the line turns westwards and runs down towards Laxey on the southern slopes of Glen Roy. Car 3 of 1893, still with bow collector, climbs the sustained 1 in 40 gradient towards South Cape soon after the opening of the extension to Laxey (Rencell Road) in 1894. Car 3 was one of several cars destroyed in the Laxey depot fire of 1930.

Car 5 and trailer climb at the same spot 65 years later. The trackside vegetation has grown, but otherwise the scene is largely unchanged, and houses on Glen Road in the bottom of the valley can be identified. A power station was built some distance below the line in 1899 to provide additional current for the extended route. Today it is hard to imagine that the valley gardens were once a hive of industrial activity connected with the mines. *M&P/ADP*

The first depot at Laxey, designed to house 16 cars, was built in 1894, but was destroyed by fire in 1930, with the loss of 11 cars and trailers. It was rebuilt promptly on the same site, close to the location of the original Laxey terminus at Rencell Road. Access is via a trailing connection from the running line (right); this leads to a head-shunt, from which cars reverse into the shed. It appears to be a three-track shed, but in fact there is a fourth. The northernmost line (in the darkness to the left of car 29) can be reached only by passing through the depot to the far end, then reversing on to it – a very curious arrangement, which inevitably resulted in the fourth track housing little-used or withdrawn items of rolling-stock. On 29 August 1962 an open crossbench car hauling trailer 62 passes the side of the depot on its way to Laxey, while inside the shed are cars 29 and 27, waiting the call from the Laxey Station Master to collect passengers returning to Douglas from trips on the Snaefell Mountain Railway.

Laxey shed has housed some unusual items over the years. In August 1998 IMR locomotive No 1 *Sutherland* was a temporary resident while allocated to haul special steam trips between Laxey and Dhoon on the electric line. *Both EG*

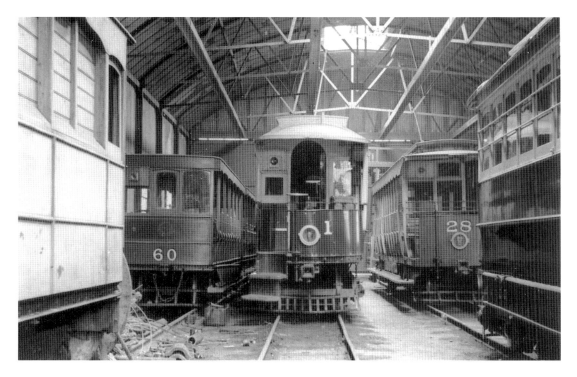

The fourth track in Laxey Depot is visible on the left in this 1956 view, accommodating two open trailers and one of the disused 10-13 series of 1895 power cars, which had seen little service, been stored for many years, and was then converted into a freight trailer in 1918. Car 1 sits on the third track and cars 28 and 2 are on line 2.

At the time of writing Laxey Depot lies empty and roofless, its condition deplorable, the precious items of rolling-stock stored elsewhere, future uncertain. The present Minister of the Department of Tourism & Leisure has approved the rebuilding of the structure in similar form to the original, so it is hoped that it will once again serve its purpose as a useful and secure depot midway along the line. In May 2006 it housed only a tower wagon, a flat truck, and a track-ballasting machine. Through the open doorway at the rear may be glimpsed the wall of the Laxey sub-station. It is through this door that the short head-shunt lies, which enables rolling-stock to reach track 4. *ADP/EG*

Above Beyond Laxey Depot building lay the 1894 terminus, a temporary arrangement until Glen Roy could be bridged and the line could enter the area that forms the present interchange with the Snaefell Mountain Railway. Passengers on the electric railway do not always realise that in entering Laxey they are passing over a splendid viaduct – only when viewed from below does one gain some idea of its height, and the difficulty that must have been experienced in its construction. The view has not changed very much since its completion. *EG*

Middle and bottom Crossing the viaduct in 1999, open crossbench car 16 is hauling two trailers, a highly unusual occurrence, during an enthusiasts' week. Saloon 19, running without a trailer, was the sole car working the lightly loaded winter service when photographed from the same viewpoint on 3 March 2007. *Both EG*

Above At the north end of Glen Roy viaduct the MER lines are set through the former churchyard to the Mines Tavern (ex-Station Hotel), an area that until the 1890s formed the garden of Mines Captain Reddicliffe, whose house survives in part as the public house. Crossbench car 27, shutters closed and fitted with non-standard vestibule, was serving as the engineering department's car when captured on film in 1998 nearing the end of the viaduct. Car 26 waits with a trailer ready to depart on a southbound service to Douglas. *EG*

Below On leaving the viaduct, the present interchange opens out to reveal on the left the terminal tracks of the Snaefell Mountain Railway, scene of special celebrations in 1998, when this line-up of three No 1s was arranged: Snaefell car 1 on the left, IMR No 1 *Sutherland* in the centre, and MER No 1 on the right. *EG*

The picture postcard view of Laxey dating from the early 1900s includes a rare view of the MER's Bonner patent road-rail wagons being towed by a 14-18 class crossbench car. Three Bonner wagons were acquired for freight work in 1899, and remained in use until 1914. To the right is the impressive refreshment room of 1899, which was destroyed by fire in 1917.

The second view is another picture postcard, this time from the 1930s (and still on sale in the 1950s), illustrating the 1899 booking office and waiting room, with 'LAXEY' outlined in white letters on the roof, and one of the two rustic sales kiosks. Car 7, with trailer and goods van attached, waits on the MER southbound departure line for holidaymakers returning from the Snaefell Mountain Railway. The station area itself is some 100 feet above sea level, and a walk down the harbour at Old Laxey can take in the glen gardens, once the ore-washing floors of the former lead mines.

On 24 May 1985, the date of the third picture, Snaefell Mountain Railway car 5 waits for the Station Master's permission to commence the journey to the summit, while MER car 6, on a short working to Laxey, has just delivered many of the Snaefell passengers. Having reversed around its trailer, the MER car is about to propel it to the goods shed siding, there to wait for another load of visitors returning to Douglas. Car 6 is hiding the ticket office and waiting room, but part of the rustic kiosk may be seen. Note the title of the undertaking at this date appears as 'Isle of Man Passenger Transport'. The one-piece windscreen contrasts with the original split screen on car 7 in the previous illustration.

Finally car 2 of 1893 with trailer 42 waits at this timeless spot on 7 June 2006. The station buildings now contain a café, and the conservatory-like extension is the Station Master's office. Laxey remains the busiest halt on the system, and the Station Master is also responsible for dispatching the Snaefell cars. The MER has thoughtfully provided a number of bench seats, making it a very pleasant spot from which to watch the world go by!
Commercial postcards (2)/EG (2)

Crossbench car 32 and trailer 61 arrive in Laxey in May 1985 carry the green and white livery that was adopted for a brief period in 1957-58 when the MER was first nationalised. Afterwards, repaints reverted to the traditional colours, though both 32 and 61 reappeared briefly in green and white as a reminder of past liveries.

Winter saloon 20 sports the more austere 'economy livery' as it arrives at the same spot 20 years later in May 2005, the company title being abbreviated merely to 'M.E.R'. The 3ft 6in-gauge tracks of the Snaefell line's terminal stubs are in the foreground of both pictures. *Both EG*

The track layout within Laxey station has some interesting features. The two MER tracks (left) have two crossovers to enable cars terminating at Laxey to run round the trailer with the minimum of effort. The power car leaves its trailer, moves forward, then reverses over the northernmost link to the adjoining track, passing alongside its trailer as it does so. The trailer brake is then released, and the vehicle rolls by gravity (assisted by muscle power) over the southernmost link, to be attached to the rear of the towing car, ready for the return to Douglas. On the right are the wider tracks of the Snaefell line, linked to the MER metals by a dual-gauge connection installed in 1932 to allow Snaefell cars to be maintained and painted at Derby Castle. To do this, bodies were lifted and placed on accommodation trucks to be towed over the dual-gauge link, and thence to Douglas. Car 14 is seen alongside the northernmost crossover on 27 May 1981, while engaged on engineering department duties propelling a goods van with tower attached.

Winter saloon 19 sits over the points of the southernmost crossover on 1 April 2003, with the dual-gauge connection to the Snaefell line on the right. The Snaefell tracks are 6 inches wider than the MER's 3-foot gauge. The third rail is apparent on the extreme right. *EG/AKK*

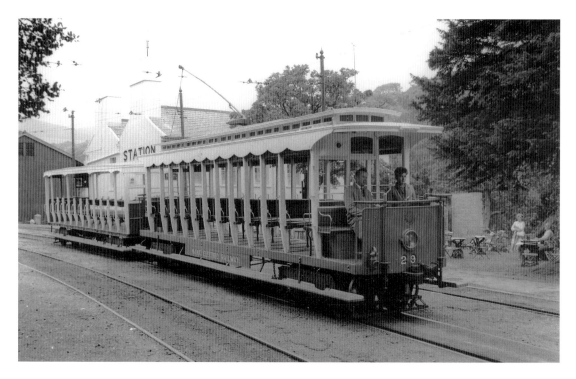

The ratchet cars rely for their braking power on the hand-brake only, and are not fitted with air-brakes. Consequently, although perfectly safe, they are rarely in use today. However, when visitors to the Isle of Man were more numerous, they were usually in evidence working the extra services, as occasion demanded, between Douglas and Laxey. Here the crew of car 29 are waiting on the centre track at Laxey beside the Station Hotel (now the Mines Tavern) for a southbound service car from Ramsey to pass, before using the crossover.

In the second picture the driver of car 28 gently releases the hand-brake as he moves off from the same spot on 28 August 1962. At this period the khaki dustcoat seemed to be the regular uniform issue for tramcar crew members. The Station Hotel was once owned by the MER, but was sold off in 1957. *ADP/EG*

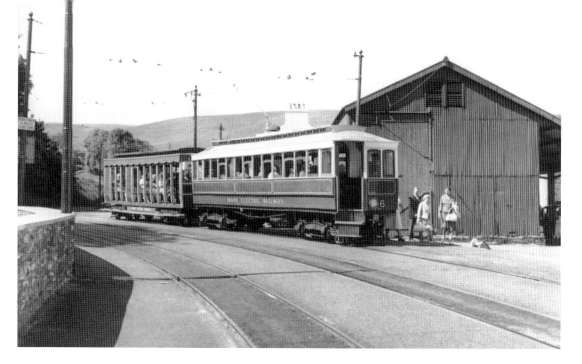

At the north end of Laxey interchange, three tracks lead out to the road crossing. That on the left is the Snaefell line, single-only until doubled on the far side of the road, while the other two are the MER lines. On the right is the MER goods shed, dating from 1903, which has a siding alongside as well as a single track leading into the building. Car 6 arrives with a well-loaded service from Ramsey on the 29 June 1965.

In a scene largely unchanged, Car 2 with trailer 42 passes the same spot on 7 June 2006. The Douglas to Laxey section is the busiest length of the line, carrying many passengers who transfer to the Snaefell Mountain Railway, but those who do not venture further than Laxey miss the scenic splendours of the northern section. *Both EG*

The short siding alongside the goods shed has traditionally been used to stable a car set on stop-over time on the extra workings to Laxey, while waiting for passengers returning from Snaefell. It has also seen use for storage of assorted permanent way materials, and for some time was home to converted trailer 52. Car 14 is on permanent way duty with a flat trailer in about 1957.

Car 32 receives attention from a crew member on the siding on 27 May 2005. The siding is now shorter than it used to be, the extremity being given over to a display of implements from the adjoining blacksmith's shop. *RFM/EG*

The ride over the northern section of the MER coastal route was nearly lost when the line between Laxey and Ramsey was closed in 1975. Fortunately, wiser counsels prevailed, and services were restored in 1977. Leaving Laxey, the tram enjoys right-of-way as it negotiates three road crossings before regaining its reserved track at an area unofficially called 'Little Egypt', a title derived from the resemblance of the spoil heaps of mine waste to desert pyramids. 'Ham and Egg Terrace' lies in the background as winter saloon 22 takes the curve at the third road crossing on 21 July 1963. The edge of the former Isle of Man Road Services bus garage may be glimpsed on the extreme right.

In a scene largely unchanged, except for road markings and the presence of parked cars outside 'Ham & Egg Terrace', winter saloon 20 makes the same journey on 8 June 2006. On the road to the 1854 'Lady Isabella' water wheel, built to pump water from the mines, the terrace gained its unusual name from the fact that housewives used to offer early morning breakfasts to miners on their way to work. *ADP/EG*

The tramcars seen in the previous illustrations have just passed over the top of the longest railway tunnel in the island. Mining at Laxey began in about 1780, and a narrow-gauge tramway was used to carry ore out of the mine to the washing floors. Wagons were hauled by ponies until 1877, when two 19-inch-gauge steam locomotives, built by Stephen Lewin of Dorset, were acquired. Named *Ant* and *Bee*, they remained in use until the mines closed in 1929. *Ant* is seen here about to enter the tunnel beneath the main Laxey-Ramsey road.

The Laxey & Lonan Heritage Trust has restored the surface section of the former tramway, re-opened the tunnel, and has commissioned two replica locomotives for use on the line. Passengers can now ride in a tiny carriage along the line where loaded wagons were once hauled from the mine, and there are demonstration runs of ore trains. The Trust has also completed another major project in the restoration and reinstatement of the Snaefell Mine Waterwheel in the valley gardens – two highly commendable achievements. *DB/EG (2)*

From Laxey the MER trams begin a long climb to the summit of the line at Ballaragh. On the way passengers can enjoy spectacular views of the coastline and, on clear days, may see the Cumbrian hills across the water. The cliff-side section by Bulgham Bay was the scene of a difficulty in 1967, when a section of the embankment wall collapsed, and services had to be divided until repairs were complete. Car 14 and flat trailer, on works duty, are seen here at work south of the slip in July 1967. What appears to be half a shed was acting as a station master's hut.

Winter saloon 21 and trailer 41 approach the summit on the 7 June 2006. This length of straight track usually features the longest stretch of non-stop running on the system, for cars are rarely halted before Dhoon Glen. Early publicity for the line advertised 'Invigorating Trips on the Open Cars' or 'Health-Giving Sea and Mountain Breezes', claims to which riders on the open cars or trailers will testify. *ADP/EG*

The spectacular coastal scenery of the northern section becomes ever more apparent as the line nears the summit. Winter saloon 19 and trailer 40 are heading southwards down the steep gradient of 1 in 24 with a service from Ramsey in 1995. Note the full company title carried by the tram here: 'The Manx Electric Railway Co Ltd'.

An unchanging scene has car 5 and trailer 43 heading southwards on 7 June 2006, passing a dual-purpose bus and tram stop sign by the roadside. Passengers on this length of track are often entertained by the sight of a herd of wild goats that inhabit this part of the island, and often stray on to the line. *Both EG*

The highest point on the line is reached on the sharp curve at Ballaragh ('Place of the Rocks'), 588 feet above sea level. At this point the line takes a westerly bend as it changes to a falling gradient on the southern slopes of Dhoon Glen.

Except for the variations in painting styles on the tramcars, the scene has changed hardly at all since the line was opened to Ramsey in 1899. The evening sun glints on the waters of the Irish Sea as car 21 and trailer 43 pass by with the last car of the day from Douglas on 7 September 2006. A plaque fixed to the rock face midway round the curve is in memory of the late motorman A. M. (Mike) Goodwyn, Chairman of the Manx Electric Railway Society, who worked tirelessly to promote the MER. Mike was often the driver of the first car out of Ramsey on the morning service, and would often halt the car at this point and descend from the controls armed with brush and grease pot, with which he would lubricate the rails to stop the car wheels squealing on the tight curve. *Both EG*

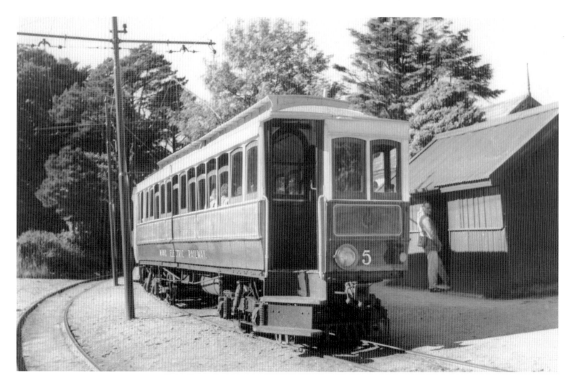

A popular stopping place for walkers visiting the picturesque glen, Dhoon Glen halt is situated on a right-hand curve as the line turns north. Tunnel car 5 was southbound when photographed on 29 June 1965. Off the picture to the left was once a large hotel and refreshment room, owned by the MER, but sadly destroyed by fire in April 1932. Refreshments have since been available at a small café, situated behind the shelter, in premises leased from the Forestry Board.

Forty-one years later car 5 halts again at the same spot. The original waiting room was demolished in 1985, and replaced by a new one in 1987. The site of the former hotel is now a car park. The café continues to provide refreshments in high season, and does well in the motor cycle TT race weeks providing breakfasts for bikers. *Both EG*

The track layout at Dhoon Quarry is a reminder of the days when the tramway handled a large quantity of freight, not least stone from the two quarries at Dhoon, which remained in business until the 1930s. The site included a weighbridge, smithy, loading dock, crusher, an aerial ropeway from the Highways Board's quarry, and a narrow-gauge rail connection to the MER's own quarry. Winter saloon 22, hauling trailer 48, has just passed through the complex on a service to Ramsey in July 1972. The building (centre left) was the former creosoting shed (for dealing with railway sleepers), known as 'Creosote Cottage', and behind the photographer were more sidings containing permanent way materials.

'Creosote Cottage' was demolished during a general clearing-up of the site in 1979-80. Piles of new sleepers occupy its place on 7 June 2006 as car 6 with trailer 40 passes by on a southbound service from Ramsey. Flat trailer 45 lies on one of the sidings, evidently in use to carry ballast for the works department. *Both EG*

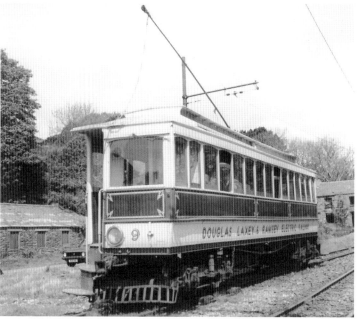

The Dhoon Quarry sidings were often a repository for unwanted items of rolling-stock, and for many years the body of one of the 10-13 series converted freight cars lay mouldering beside 'Creosote Cottage' until removed in the late 1950s.

Car 9, then in one of the historic liveries, was the occupant of a siding on 24 May 1981, though in this instance it was on a special working, and had been removed from the main running line to allow a service car to pass. To the left of the tram is the smithy, behind which the narrow-gauge connection ran into a short tunnel beneath the Ramsey road.

Signs of winter track re-laying activities are in evidence on 19 March 2006, with car 7, in deplorable state, attached to a ballast hopper wagon, and a diesel locomotive belonging to the contractor waiting the call to the work site. *TL/EG (2)*

North of Dhoon Quarry the MER line enters a beautiful stretch of countryside, with numerous farm crossings and the hills of the North Barrule dominating the scene. In 1995 winter saloon 22 is southbound from Ramsey at Ballelin in this timeless setting.

Nowadays the open cars do not often venture as far as Ramsey, except in the height of the season, or perhaps in TT race week, when the Ramsey Sprint event often results in the MER's busiest day of the year, bringing bikers from Douglas. Crossbench car 32 and trailer 61 are carrying a full load on 7 June 2006. *Both EG*

One of the loveliest areas of the northern section is reached around Ballafayle, as the line passes through attractive farmland, with picture-postcard views of Maughold Head and its pristine white lighthouse in the distance. Car 33 and matching trailer pass southwards through a leafy setting. For a time, car 33 ran with varnished pillars, though it has now reverted to the traditional white uprights. With car 32, it dates from 1906, the final purchase of MER rolling-stock. The pair celebrated their centenary in 2006, and remain the most powerful and fastest cars in the fleet.

The same location on 8 June 2006 includes a glimpse of the sea as car 20 heads for Douglas with the last service of the day from Ramsey. The main change is the evidence of improved trackwork, newly laid and ballasted during the winter of 2005-06. *Both EG*

At Belle Vue halt the signboard invites passengers to alight and visit Port-e-Vullen. The wide sweep of Ramsey Bay, the Queen's Pier and the northern plains are visible as the cliff-edge route drops towards the town. Car 21, climbing from Ramsey on 8 July 1960, passes the small hut that once served as a shelter as it crosses the minor road to Maughold Village. At this time waiting passengers could enjoy an uninterrupted view across the water.

By 9 June 2006, as car 5 heads a Douglas-bound service, the vegetation has proliferated to such an extent that it all but obscures the view in front of the new shelter. *ADP/EG*

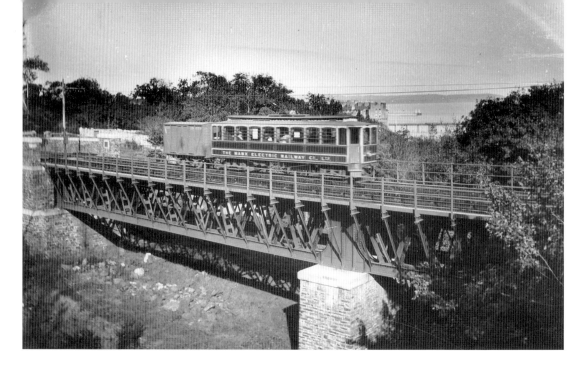

Construction of the line to Ramsey reached the outskirts of the town in August 1898, with a temporary terminus at Ballure. The fare from Douglas was then 3s 6d return (17½p in today's money). The last great obstacle to entering the town proper was the deep ravine of Ballure Glen, which was successfully spanned in 1899 with a steel bridge designed by William Knowles and erected by Francis Morton & Company of Garston, Liverpool. A winter saloon of the 19-22 series, complete with goods van, crosses the bridge as it leaves Ramsey with a Douglas-bound service in the early 1900s. A section of the pier and the harbour entrance lights may be noted in the distance.

The growth of vegetation now prevents a similar view, but car 21 is in the identical position as it works southwards on 22 July 2006. Trams are restricted to a maximum speed of 5mph when crossing the bridge.
Commercial postcard/EG

From Ballure the MER takes a back-road route into Ramsey via Walpole Road (named after a Lieutenant Governor), and where until 1995 the only example of grooved tramway rail could be seen, a reminder of the never-fulfilled intention to surface the reserved track area. Winter saloon 20, towing a goods van, makes its way southwards over the roadside section at Walpole Road on 21 May 1956. This section of track had evidently escaped the attention of the weed-killing staff.

Fifty years on, tunnel car 6 is at the same location, hauling trailer 40 on the first service of the day from Ramsey on 7 June 2006. The gable-end of the house on the right may be identified, but the grooved rail has gone, and the style of motor car has changed. *RFM/EG*

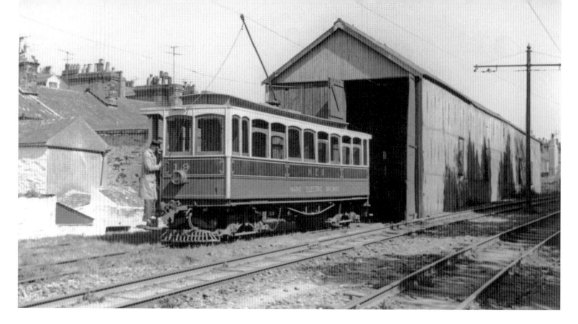

The Ramsey tram shed was erected in 1898 alongside the temporary terminus at Ballure, on the present site of the Ballure Gardens. It was designed to house six tramcars, with inspection pits for three. In 1899 it was dismantled and re-erected on its present site by Parsonage Road. It has two tracks, the first of which is reached from the southbound line. The more inaccessible second track (the 'back road') is gained only via a head-shunt from the first track, and so is often used to store the less frequently needed items of rolling-stock. The first track is normally used to stable the cars scheduled to work the early morning duty out of Ramsey. Winter saloon 19 enters the depot after working the last service of the day from Douglas on 21 May 1961.

For a time the depot housed a selection of museum exhibits, until the goods shed was converted for that purpose in 1979, and it remains as a store for unused cars and trailers, as well as serving as a running shed for the Ramsey-based service car. For the current timetable only one car set is required to be stabled overnight at Ramsey. Ratchet car 18, on a rare outing, was shunting the passenger car from the defunct Ramsey Pier Tramway when caught on film in 1999. More recently some redundant items have been stored elsewhere, and space made for outside contractors to use the shed for repainting cars. *ADP/EG*

The view from Ramsey Depot entrance on 24 May 1981 shows car 20, newly arrived from Douglas, waiting by the points of the cattle-dock siding for the Station Master's permission to proceed across Parsonage Road into the terminus. On the terminal stub the conductor of car 2 is placing the trolley on the overhead wire as it moves to collect a trailer on the departure line. In the centre foreground is the connecting track to the depot head-shunt, and (extreme right) the further connection from the head-shunt to the second depot track – evidently little used and, in any event, obstructed by the parked vehicles. The building behind the lorry was the 1897 Palace Concert Hall (latterly the Plaza Cinema), once owned by the MER but sold in 1938.

The cinema was demolished in 1991, and the track for the former cattle dock was removed in recent years. The depot trackwork remains the same, however. It is 9.40am on 7 June 2006 and car 6 has hauled trailer 40 from the shed, and has used the nearby crossovers to run round and take up position at the Douglas end. Meanwhile, the trailer, aided by a favourable gradient and with the conductor at the brake wheel, is rolling gently into the terminus, followed by car 6, ready to hook-up and prepare for the 10.10 departure. *Both EG*

The terminal layout at Ramsey consisted of a spur into the goods shed (left), with a siding alongside, together with the main arrival and departure tracks, linked by a crossover (centre right). In this 1947 view crossbench car 25, with trailer and van, sits on the departure line, while trailer 55 and another crossbench car wait in reserve beside the goods shed, where van 12 fills the doorway.

The layout today remains the same, though the goods shed is now home to a Youth Club, and the siding (still equipped with its overhead wire) has inexplicably been rendered unusable by the placing of two large flower tubs across the track. The procedure for power cars to run round their trailers at Ramsey is for the car set to come to a halt on the Douglas side of the crossover. The power car uncouples, moves forward, then reverses over to the adjoining track. The conductor, or Station Master, releases the trailer brake and allows it to roll by gravity to a point beyond the crossover, from where it is collected again by the towing car. *RP/EG*

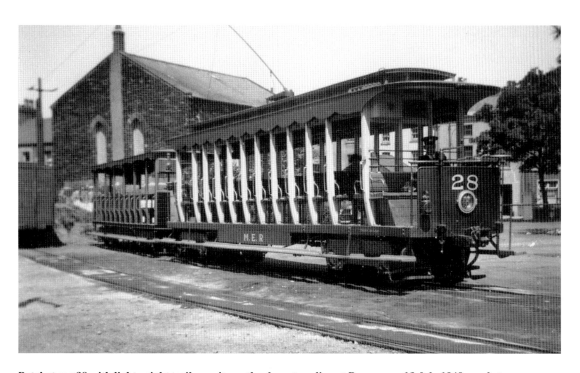

Ratchet car 28 with lightweight trailer waits on the departure line at Ramsey on 12 July 1949, ready to commence the 17¾-mile journey to Douglas, which will take it 1 hour and 15 minutes. The use of oil lamps on the dash plates to supplement the electric lighting was required by statute, and the practice continued until 1987-88, by which time the oil lamps were deemed unnecessary. Behind the trailer is Quayles Hall, built as a result of an 1830 petition for a Presbyterian Church for the many Scots who had settled in Ramsey.

Ramsey was favoured with a new station building in 1964, which incorporated waiting room, toilets, booking office, Station Master's room and crews' refreshment facilities. The edge of this building may be seen on the right, adorned with bunting for a special occasion – the celebration of the centenary of the Ramsey line in 1999. One of the two surviving original cars from 1893 is in evidence – a remarkable survival. One wonders how many times it must have made the Douglas-Ramsey journey. *DB/EG*

The Snaefell Mountain Railway

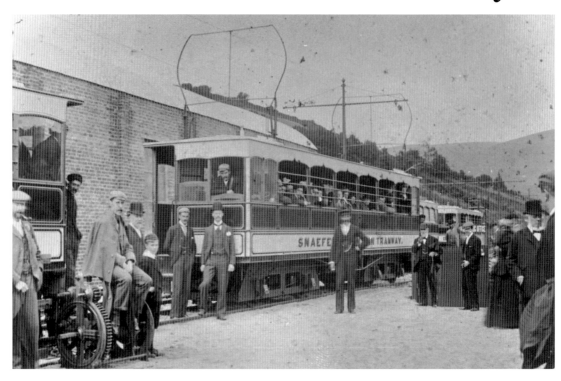

The 5-mile line from Laxey to the summit of Snaefell, 2,036 feet above sea level, was completed in 1895. A gauge of 3ft 6in was selected, the extra 6 inches accommodating a centrally placed Fell Patent rail, which could be gripped by a calliper brake when the cars were descending steep inclines. Six tramcars, originally unglazed except for the end platforms, were supplied by G. F. Milnes of Birkenhead, with electrical equipment provided by Mather & Platt. The original terminus at Laxey was alongside the car shed, reached by a flight of steps from 'Ham & Egg Terrace'. This is the opening day, 21 August 1895.

After the terminus was re-sited to form the interchange with the MER, the line at the side of the depot became the repository for assorted items of rolling-stock, including on 21 May 1959 the unused and semi-derelict body of open freight car No 7 ('Maria'), the tower wagon, and the open truck. Car 4 beyond was at this date in the unpopular green livery. *M&P/ADP*

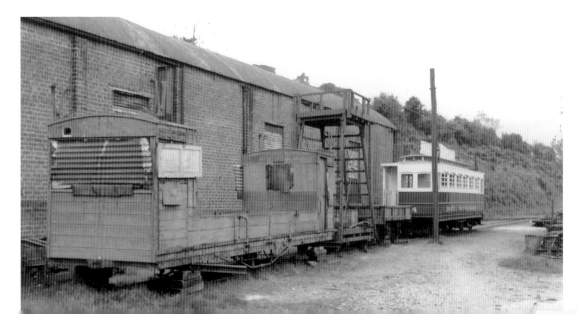

Snaefell cars are usually dispatched from the Laxey interchange at half-hourly intervals from 10.30am in the season, according to demand. The journey to the summit takes 30 minutes. The Snaefell cars retained a sprung version of the Hopkinson bow collector, as it was better able to maintain contact with the overhead wire in the high winds sometimes experienced on the mountain. The roof-boards above the clerestory read 'THIS CAR GOES TO THE SUMMIT OF SNAEFELL. FINE VIEW OF BIG WHEEL. HOTEL AND REFRESHMENT ROOMS ON SUMMIT OF MOUNTAIN'.

The roof-boards were removed after 1970, when a fire severely damaged car 5 – it was thought that rocking in the mountain winds might have caused frayed cables. Three Snaefell cars, Nos 2, 5 and 1, wait at Laxey for passengers arriving on the MER tracks (right) on 30 April 2007, the first day of the operating season. Five of the six cars are normally available for service, while the sixth undergoes annual maintenance. *ADP/EG*

The half-way point of the mountain railway is reached at 'The Bungalow', the crossing point of the TT racing circuit, where there is a short accommodation siding and an intermediate booking office, for here is the only stopping point en route. In the centenary year, 1995, the Bungalow Station Master was resplendent in gold-braided uniform. After the 1970 fire, car 5 was rebuilt, and as a result looks somewhat different from its fellows, having lost its clerestory roof feature, but gained bus-type windows.

The Bungalow now has a new booking office, constructed on the opposite side of the track from the older one, on the site of the 1896 Bungalow Hotel, demolished in 1958. The modern structure is complete with waiting room and associated amenities, a welcome shelter for waiting passengers in cold and windy weather. Car 2, equipped with headlight, pauses outside the new building on its upward journey on 28 September 2006, almost at the end of its operating season. *Both EG*

The SMR has always enjoyed a steady and profitable seasonal routine, usually operating from May to the end of September, and holidaymakers usually include a trip up the mountain as part of their itinerary. The turreted and castellated hotel at the upper terminus dated from 1906, and replaced an earlier refreshment room. Car 1 decants its passengers in the 1930s.

Fire gutted the summit hotel in 1982, and it was subsequently rebuilt in altered form, and has since received further refurbishment in 1995; the basic outline of the former building may be discerned in the shape of its successor. Car 5 waits at the summit on 16 September 2006. *Commercial postcard/EG*

Car 3 stands on the terminal stub at the summit outside the 1906 hotel as passengers board for the downward journey. On the left is the end of an open wagon, apparently loaded with coal. Supplies for the hotel were, and still are, carried to the summit in an open truck propelled up the mountain by the first car of the day, which also transports catering staff.

Car 5, showing off its Manx Gaelic lettering, stands at the same spot in September 2006. The last car of the day, usually late afternoon, brings back the hotel staff and any remaining passengers to Laxey. *DB/EG*

The line once had several unique items of trackwork, perhaps the most unusual being the point that led from the running line into the depot. The control lever of this point not only moved the two outer rails, but also sections of the centre Fell rail, thus giving continuous braking facility. It was replaced by a conventional point in 1985-86. Today, the oddities are represented only by this single-bladed point that remains at the convergence of the upward and downward tracks at the summit. The point is sprung open to receive cars arriving on the upward track, but is held over by the knee-high lever as downward cars join the right-hand track.

The point, now protected by barriers, is held by the summit Station Master as the conductor of car 5 keeps a careful watch as the car commences its downward journey. Right-hand running was adopted from the outset, the reason offered being that it would keep ascending cars on the soft outer edge of the formation, whereas descending cars, more liable to the risk of a runaway, would be on the harder, well-consolidated inner trackbed. Two-thirds of the formation had been cut into the hard rock of the hillside, the rest made up of loose excavated material. However, though this reasoning is valid for the lower section between Laxey and the Bungalow, it is scarcely applicable to the upper slopes, where the track follows a spiral curve to the right, and descending cars travel on the outer edge. *DB/EG (2)*

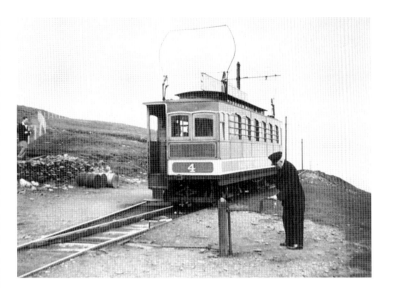

The Groudle Glen Railway

On the opening of the electric tramway as far as Groudle in 1893, entrepreneur R. M. Broadbent had already leased the narrow valley and cliff-side area with a view to developing the glen as a tourist attraction. He built a hotel, planted trees and constructed footpaths, bridges, bowling green, dance floor and even a small zoo in a rocky cove at the cliff edge, in which were seals and polar bears. To transport visitors through the glen, Broadbent conceived the idea of a 2-foot-gauge miniature railway. Locomotive *Sea Lion* and the three passenger coaches opened the service in May 1896, and in about 1898 the train has just left the Lhen Coan ('Lovely Glen') terminus, whose canopy is visible just beyond the train. The hotel appears on the skyline.

Since those first heady days the line has undergone several vicissitudes, but is now safely in the hands of the volunteers of the Isle of Man Steam Railway Supporters' Association, who operate the trains in season on Sundays, Bank Holidays and Tuesday and Wednesday evenings in July and August. Broadbent's trees have matured somewhat since 1896, as the restored *Sea Lion* leaves Lhen Coan. *V/EG*

Lime Kiln Halt, midway up the hillside at Port Groudle, where an unmade path crosses the route, is the intermediate stopping point on the three-quarter-mile route. Apart from closures during wartime, the line survived until 1962, latterly intermittently, by which time *Sea Lion* was out of service and the second locomotive, *Polar Bear* of 1902, here appearing in a fairground-type livery, was in need of major attention.

The railway lay derelict for some years, but a movement to restore the line gained momentum in 1982, resulting in partial re-opening in 1986, and culminating in complete restoration to the original terminus in 1993. Today the line is in better condition than ever before, and a new café has been built at the Sea Lion Rocks terminus. *Sea Lion* passes Lime Kiln Halt on 24 September 2006. *DB/EG*

A lengthy passing loop existed at the Headland between 1905 and 1939. From a vantage point on the main road at Howstrake, looking northwards across the Groudle inlet, the course of the line can be seen as it curves around the cliff-tops to the Sea Lion Rocks terminus, just off the top left of the picture. The café on the lower path is now but a memory.

On 24 September 2006 *Sea Lion* hauls a three-coach train returning to Lhen Coan. The train is approaching Lime Kiln Halt, the location of which is indicated by the white painted fence. The long passing loop on the Headland had been replaced by a shorter version by 1950, when the railway terminated at that point. The present loop (seen here) was installed during the renewal of trackwork in 1984. In the middle distance may be seen the new café at the Sea Lion Rocks terminus. *TL/EG*

The restored line was re-opened to the original terminus at Sea Lion Rocks in 1993, the first time trains had reached there since 1939. To achieve this, the sections of the line from the Headland had to be re-sited some yards inland, but follow the original course. Special events have included operation with visiting locomotives from other preserved lines, including the original *Polar Bear*, on loan from Amberley Chalk Pits Museum for a temporary reunion with its fellow. In the upper picture, the visiting De Winton locomotive *Chaloner* leaves Sea Lion Rocks with a train on 13 August 1995.

Richard Booth's locomotive *Annie* (a replica of a Bagnall 1911 product, completed in 1998, and a permanent resident on the line) waits at the terminal loop on 10 September 2006. The new café building (right) is the latest and welcome addition to the amenities. *All EG*

The Douglas Head
Marine Drive Tramway

The Douglas Head Marine Drive is a lasting tribute to the pioneers of a scheme of 1889 to cut and blast a ledge high on the cliff tops in order to form a road link between Douglas and the increasingly popular resort of Port Soderick, hitherto reached only by sea or steep pathway. The opening was celebrated in 1893, and a subsidiary company, the Douglas Southern Electric Tramways, was formed to construct a tramway along the landward side of the road. A single track of 4ft 8½in (the only UK standard gauge line on the island) was proposed, with a series of passing loops along the 3½-mile route. The line opened in 1896, beginning at a point above the harbour on

Douglas Head. After the flurry of new schemes in the 1890s, this proved to be the final project on the island of the Victorian transport entrepreneurs.

In the 'past' view car 7 stands at the terminus on Douglas Head in 1935. In days past, visitors often reached this point by using one of the ferries that formerly plied across the harbour, then by riding on the Douglas Head Inclined Railway. The tramway closed on the outbreak of war in 1914, but resumed operation in 1919, closing again in 1939, when the Royal Navy took over Douglas Head. Though remaining intact throughout the war, the tramway did not re-open, and in 1946 the Company Receiver disposed of the assets to the Isle of Man Highway & Transport Board. The inclined railway survived until 1953, and its course may be traced by a present-day pathway.

Of the tramway terminus no vestige remains on 10 September 2006, but the view of the Victoria Pier, the Tower of Refuge, and the sweep of Douglas Bay may be enjoyed from its former location. *RS/EG*

This page The ornamental arch of 1891 served as the toll gate, and pre-dated the tramway by some five years. The gate-keeper's house was incorporated on the seaward side of the structure. It was first proposed that the tramway should begin at the gates, but plans were altered to extend the line a short distance northwards to the Head, and for the trams to pass through the right-hand arch. Six single-truck tramcars with matching trailers were supplied for the opening of the line. Because the roadway was always on the seaward side of the line, the new cars were constructed with the trolley mast and both staircases on the landward side, making them unique. Passengers boarded and alighted only on the seaward side.

On 14 August 2006 the arch remains at the entrance to the Marine Drive, though the gate-keeper's house of the original structure has gone. The location of the turnstile may be noted on walking through the original pedestrian entrance. *AKK/EG*

The line was notable for its wild and rugged scenery, but also for the scale of its bridgework across the chasms at Pigeon's Stream (site of the power station), Wallberry and Horse Leap. Car 5, crossing the viaduct at Wallberry in 1939, is dwarfed against a backdrop of contorted layers of Manx slate.

By 6 September 2006 the viaducts at Wallberry and Horse Leap have gone, and in their place the road has been cut back into the rock face, although traces of the supports and abutments may be seen. At Pigeon's Stream, where there is a small car park, an embankment has taken the place of the bridge. The Marine Drive has reverted to the quiet and glorious isolation it knew before the line's opening in 1891. *WAC/EG*

Port Soderick, at the southern end of the line, was developing as a popular leisure centre. In 1897 the proprietors of the hotel provided a link to the tramway terminus on the cliff-top by purchasing the Falcon Cliff Hotel funicular from Douglas and re-installing it at Port Soderick. New car bodies were supplied for the re-sited lift, while the old ones became kiosks on the promenade. The pair may be discerned in front of the framework of the swing boats in the centre of the 'past' view.

   Port Soderick was all but deserted, save for the seabirds and the occasional curious visitor, in August 2006. The former route of the funicular could be followed with some difficulty, by climbing a steep and overgrown pathway to the site of the cliff-top tramway terminus. How different from the great days of the Victorian and Edwardian periods! Fortunately, car No 1 was rescued from the depot before the site was cleared in 1951, and is now preserved at the National Tramway Museum at Crich. And, of course, the splendours of the Marine Drive are still there to be enjoyed, and one can imagine what an exhilarating ride it must have been to travel over the route on the top deck of an open tram. Lovers of vintage transport may dream of such a journey in the silence and solitude of the Marine Drive, or experience the real thing on the surviving Victorian railways of the Isle of Man. *Commercial postcard/EG*

INDEX OF LOCATIONS

BIBLIOGRAPHY

Basnett, S. *The Isle of Man By Tram, Train and Foot* (Leading Edge)
Basnett, S. and Pearson, K. *Double Century* (Adam Gordon)
Boyd, J. I. C. *The Isle of Man Railway* (Oakwood Press)
Goodwyn, A. M. *Manx Electric* (Platform 5)
   Douglas Head Marine Drive & Electric Tramway (MERS)
Hendry, R. P. *The Manx Northern Railway* (Hillside)
Laxey & Lonan Heritage Trust Newsletters
Lloyd-Jones, D. *The Manx Peacocks* (Atlantic)
Manx Steam Railway News, Journal of the IoM Steam Railway Supporters' Association
Manx Transport Review, Journal of the Manx Electric Railway Society
Pearson, K. *Isle of Man Tramways* (David & Charles)
Smith, D. N. *The Groudle Glen Railway* (Plateway Press)
Three Foot, Journal of the Isle of Man Railway & Tramway Preservation Society